Sannel Larson's
Busy Bees

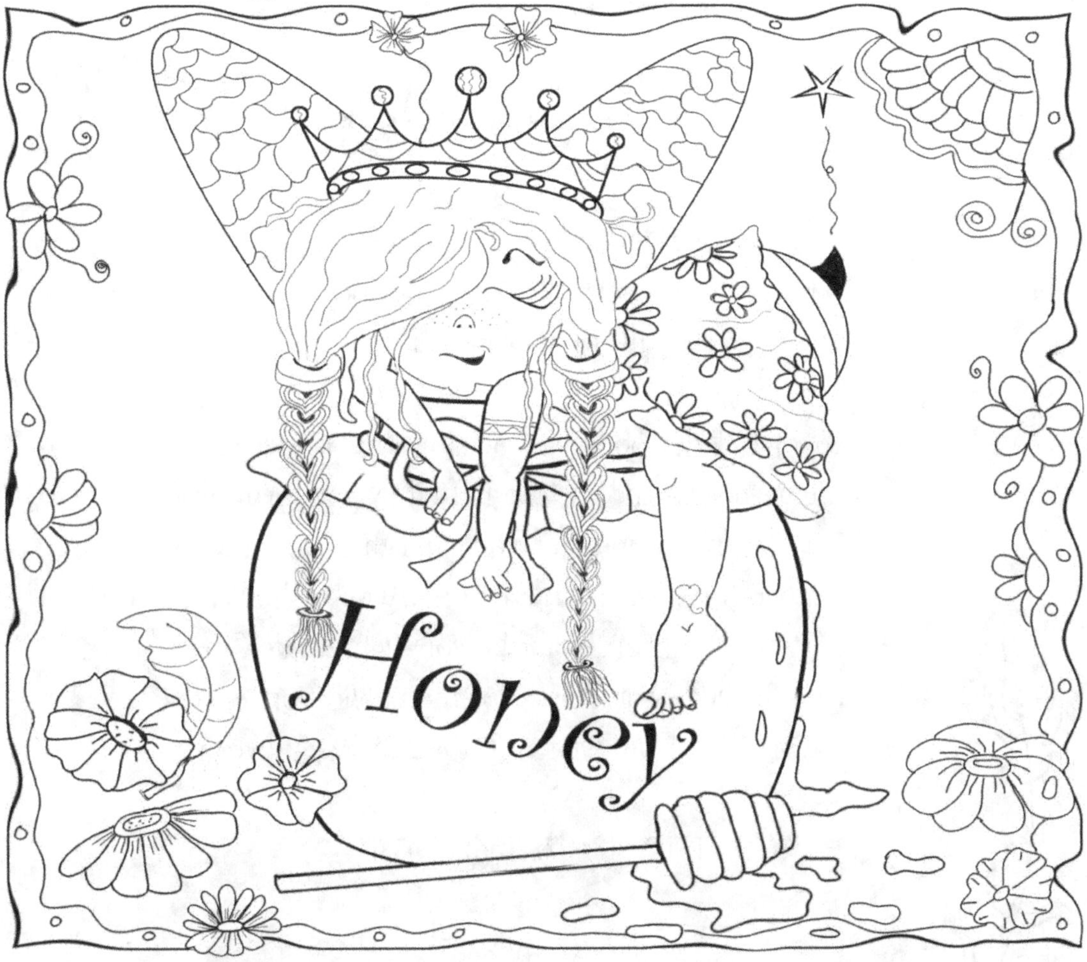

Honey

Coloring Book

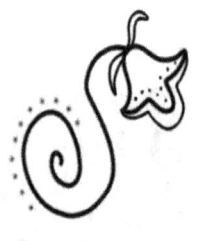

Sannel Larson's
Busy Bees
Coloring Book

ISBN-13: 978-1548885830

ISBN-10: 1548885835

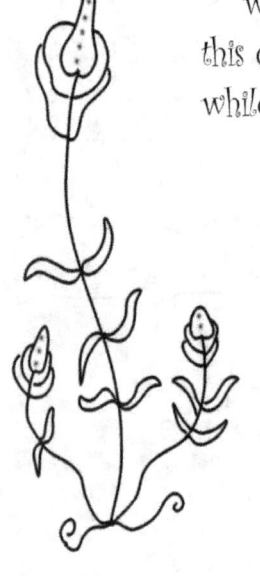

Illustrated by artist
Sannel Larson

This book belongs to:

_____

_____

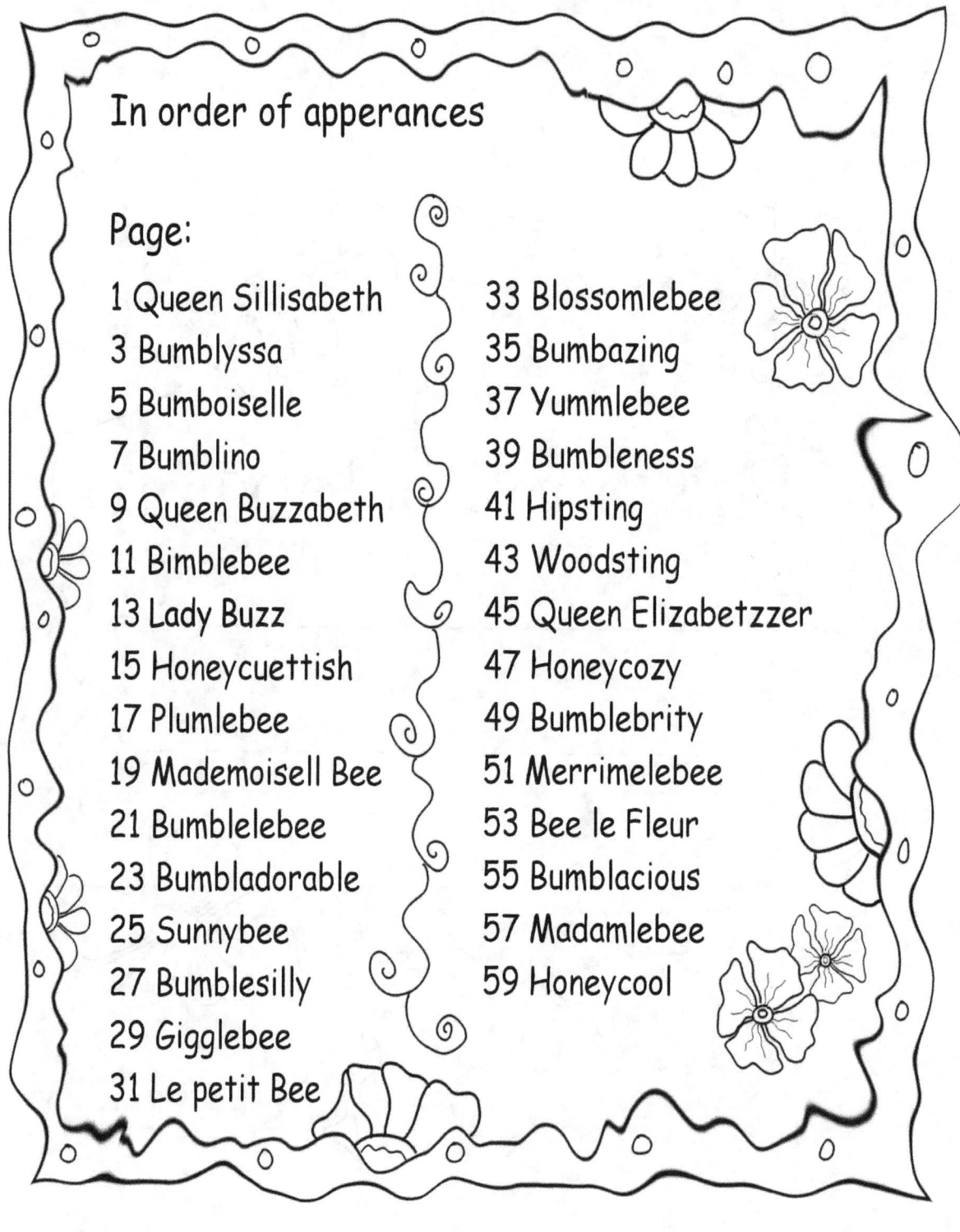

In order of apperances

Page:

A Note From The Artist...

Welcome to the Busy **Bees Coloring Book!**

Thank you to everyone for purchasing my fantasy fun coloring book. All these bumbladorable, hand-drawn illustrations for this coloring book were created with much fun, care and love. I hope you enjoy coloring it as much as I enjoyed creating it.

Please, don't forget to leave a review of this book, as well as to share your bumbazing, bee-autiful and colorful bee art on amazon.com. I would love to see Queen Sillisabeth, Queen Buzzabeth, Queen Elizabetzzer and their buzzing working girls in color.

All the illustrations are single-sided so you don't have to worry about ruining a design on the opposite page. However, I would suggest placing a piece of paper or two under the page you are coloring, and the illustration beneath will be fully protected. So go ahead and use markers, colored pencils, fine point markers, crayons and pastels.

Go ahead and use the finished pages to send to friends and family in place of "Thinking of You" cards, "Get Well" cards, or cards just to make them smile.

Happy art making everyone!

Sannel

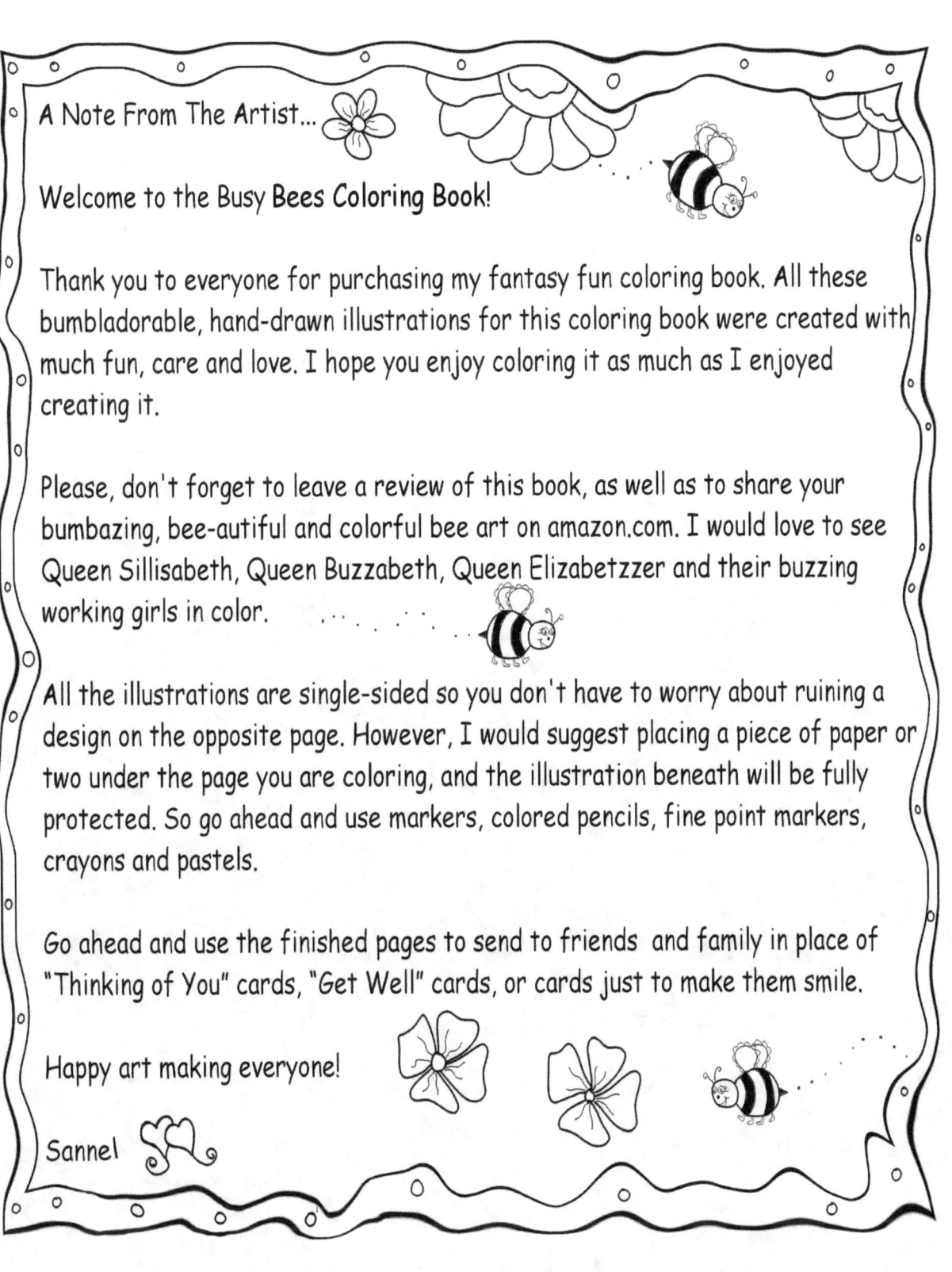

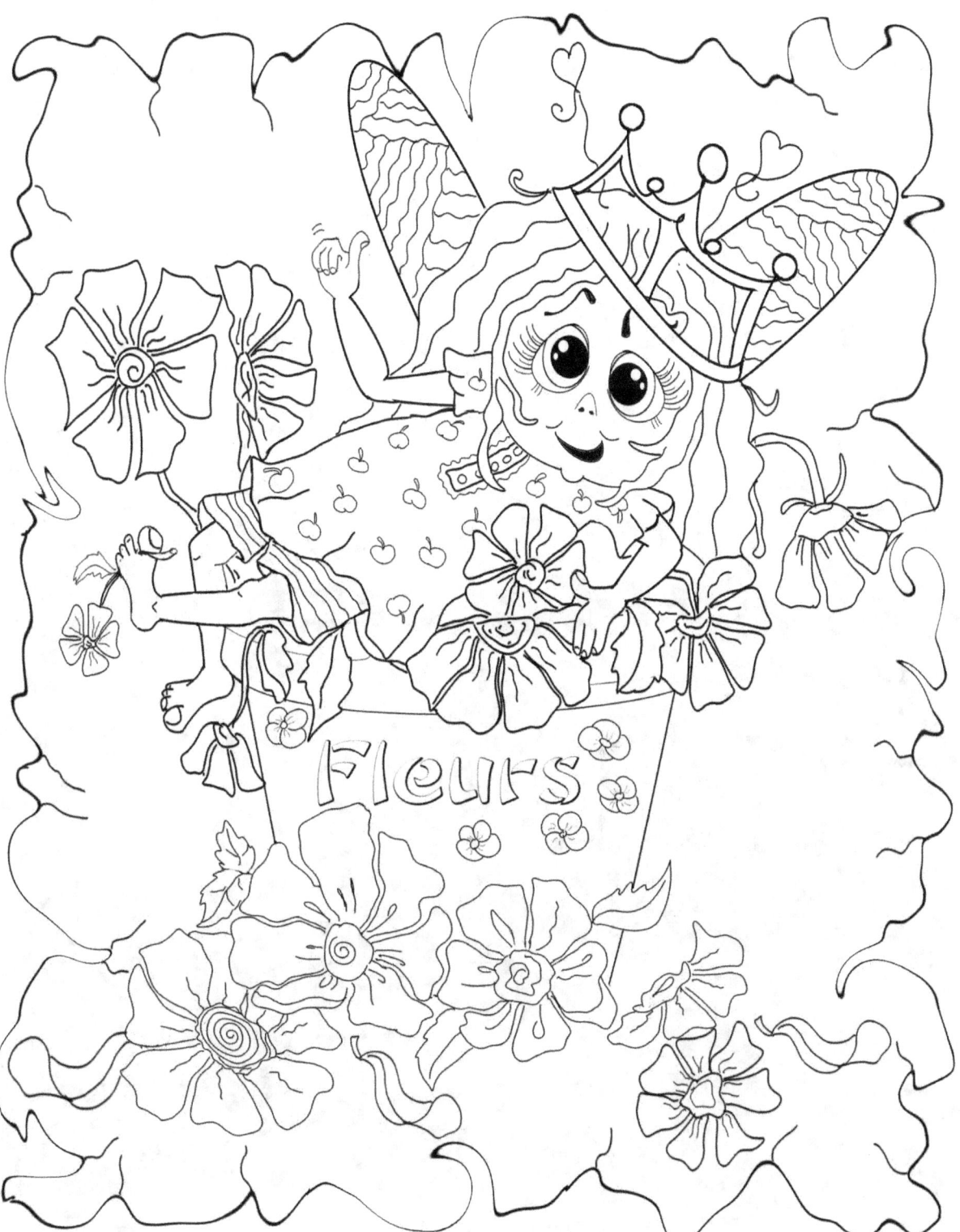

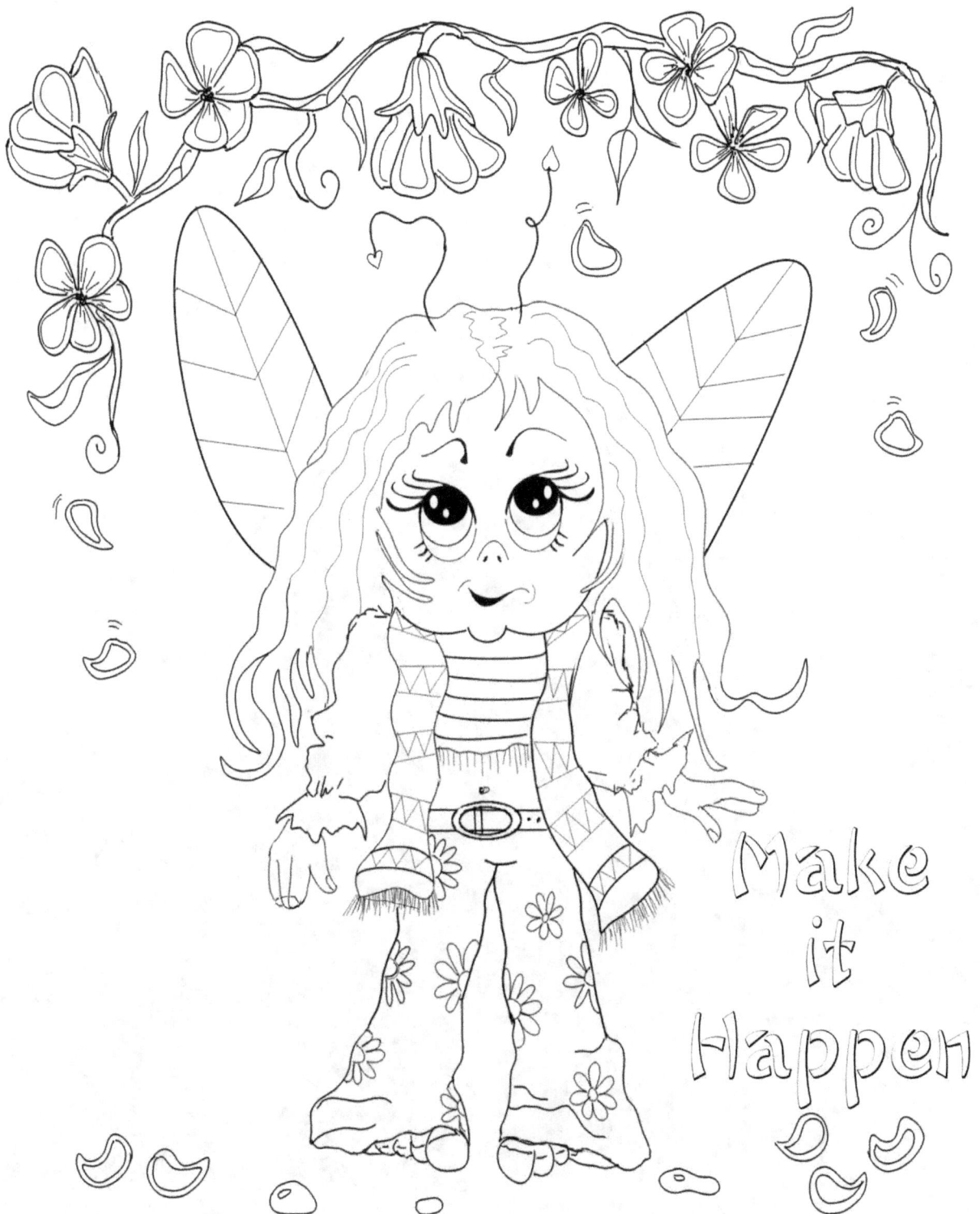

Make it Happen

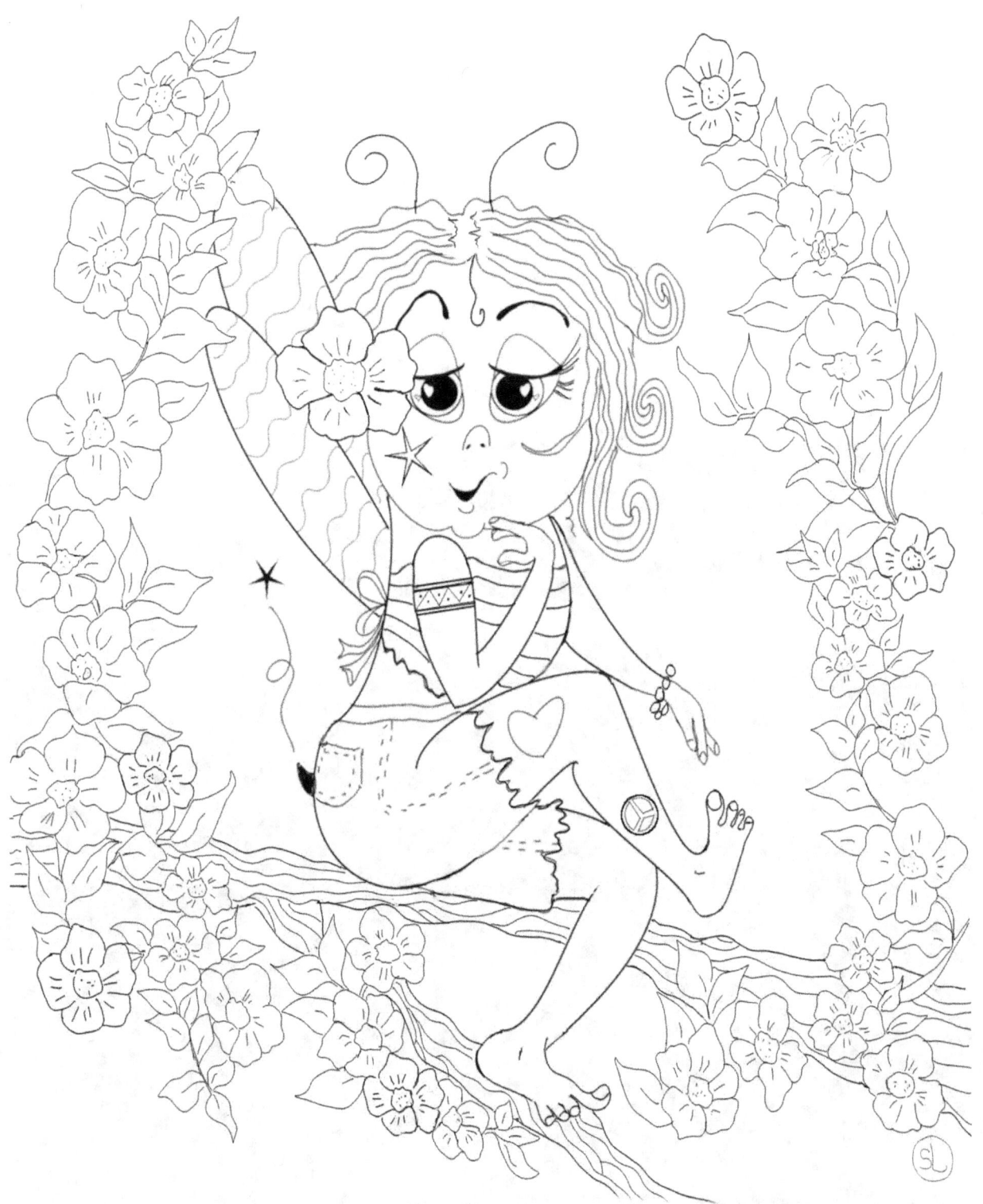

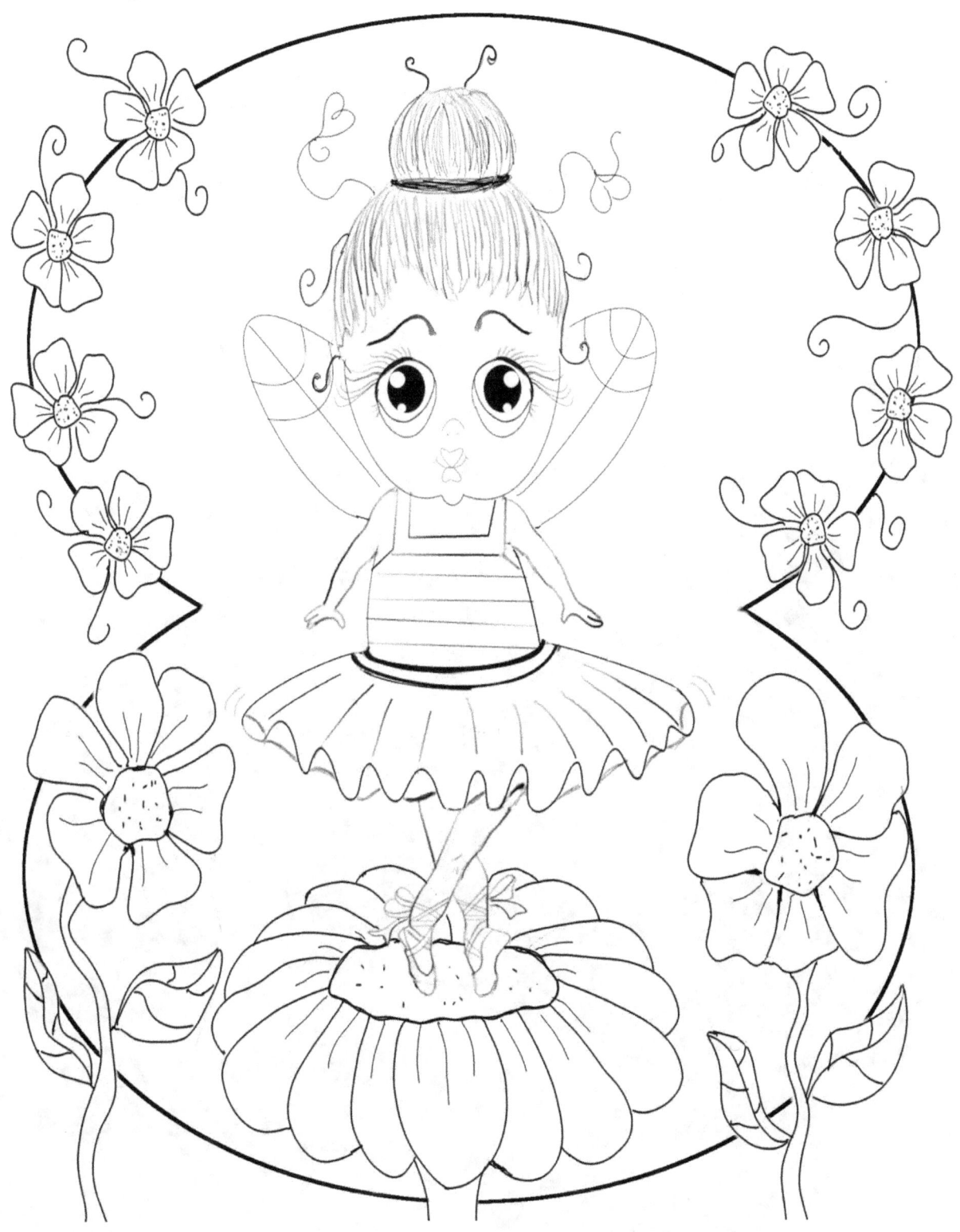

7

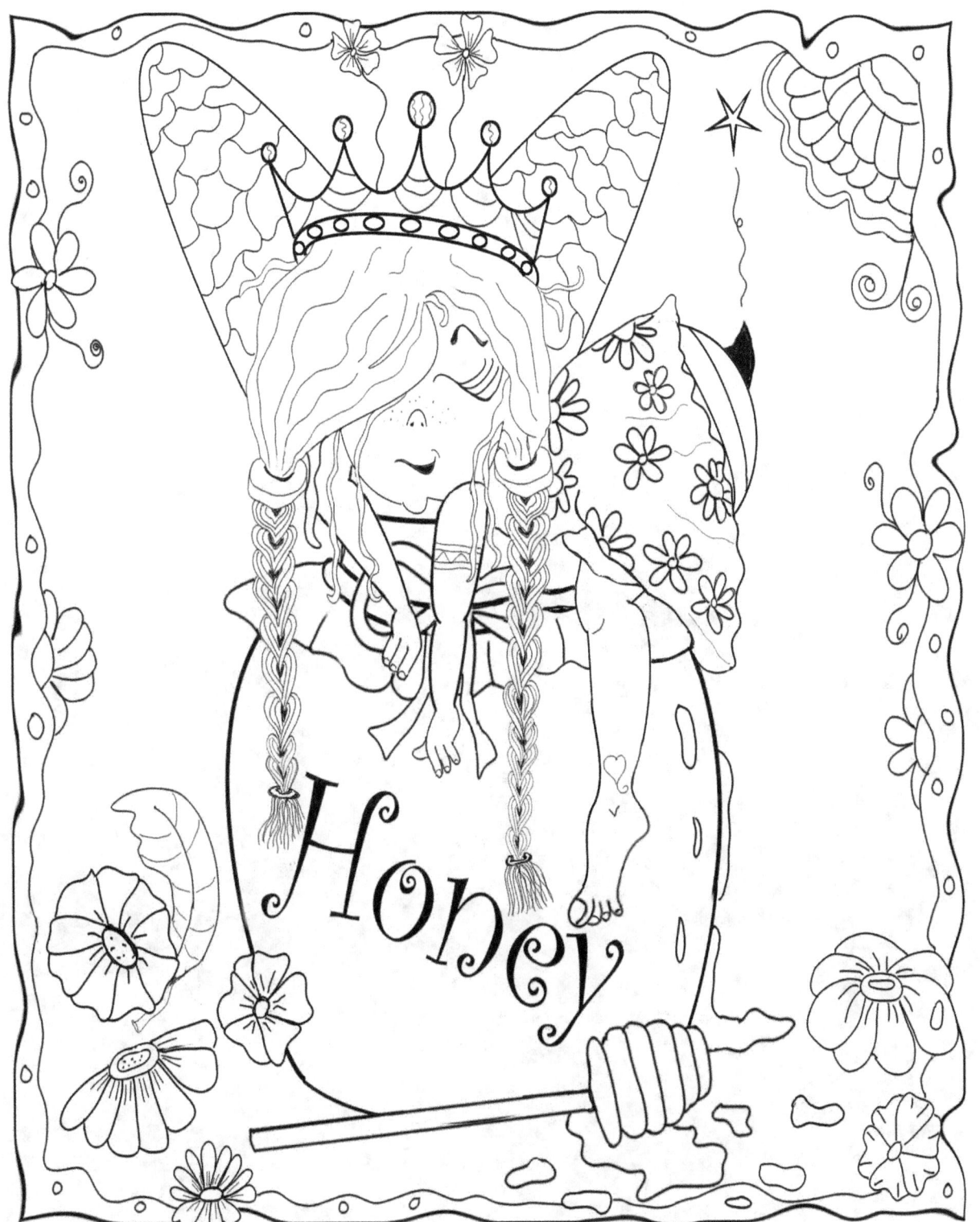

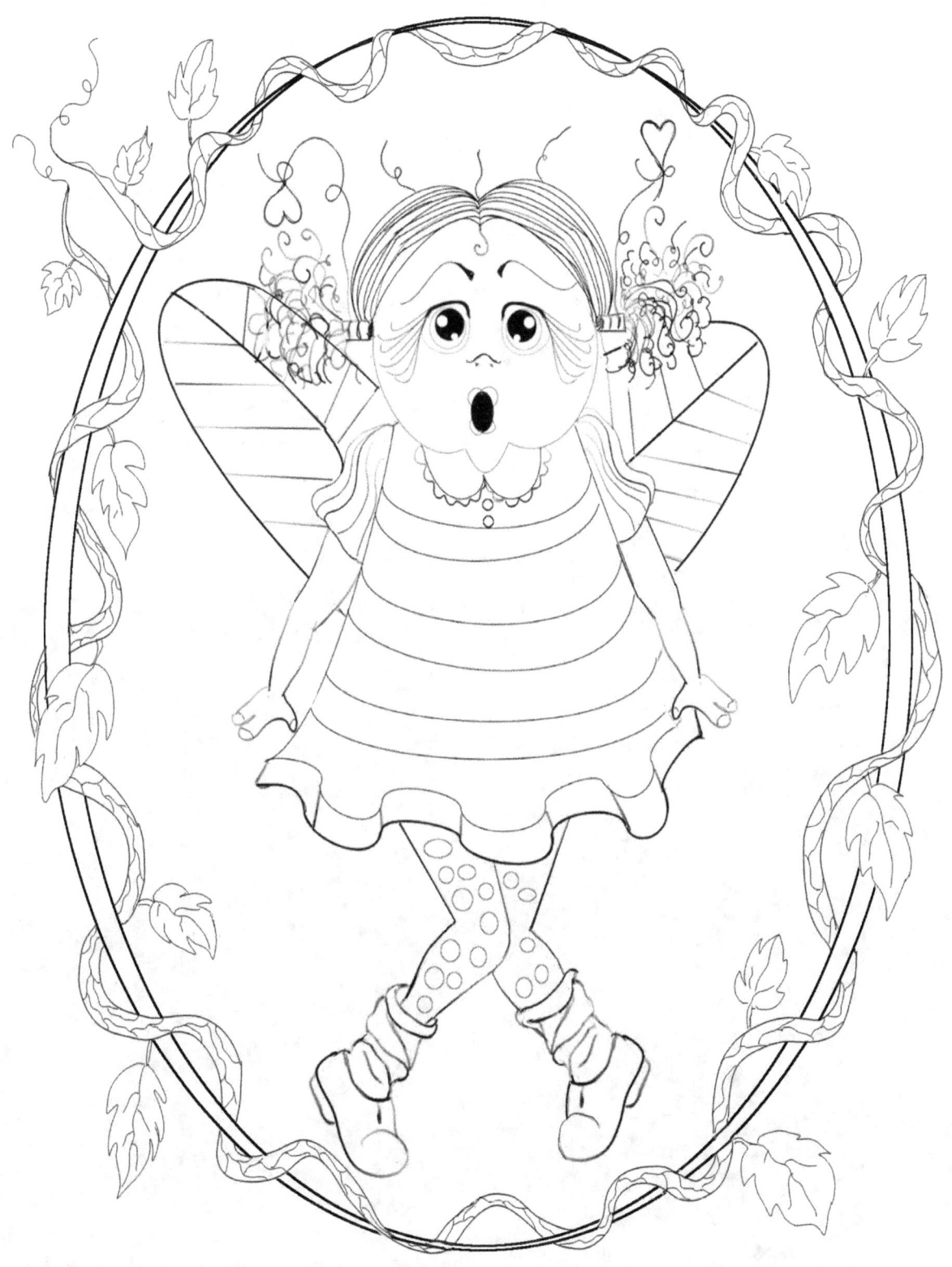

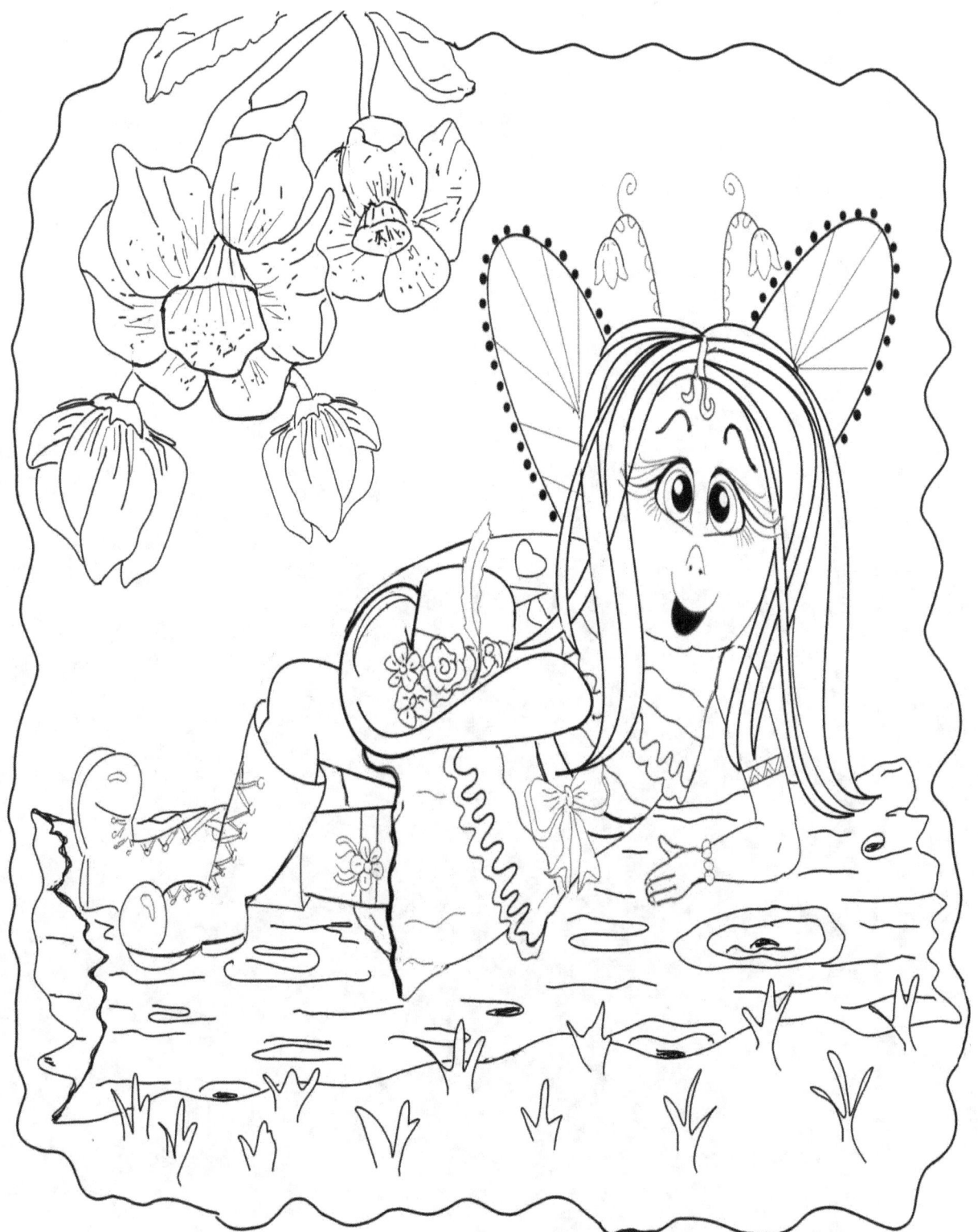

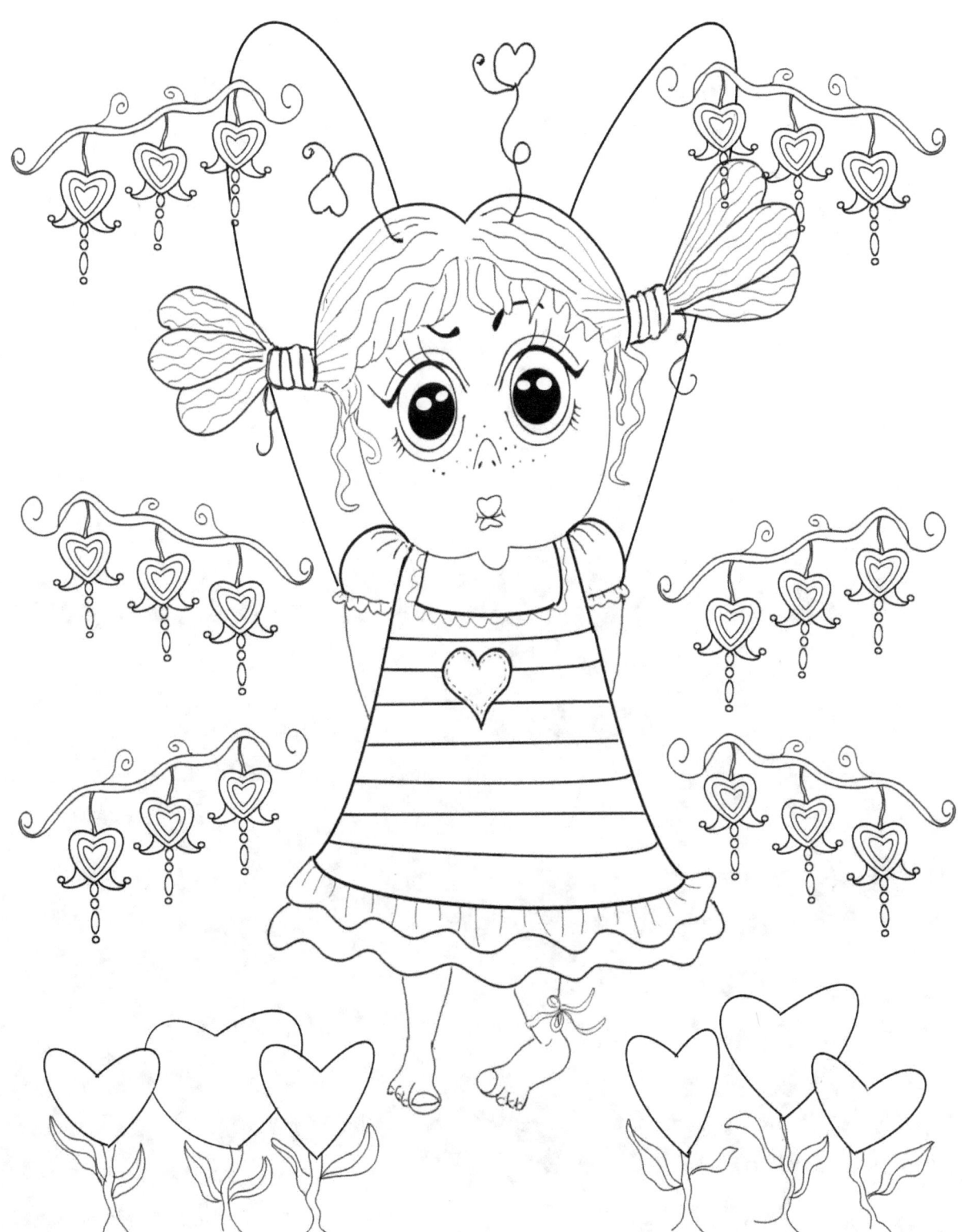

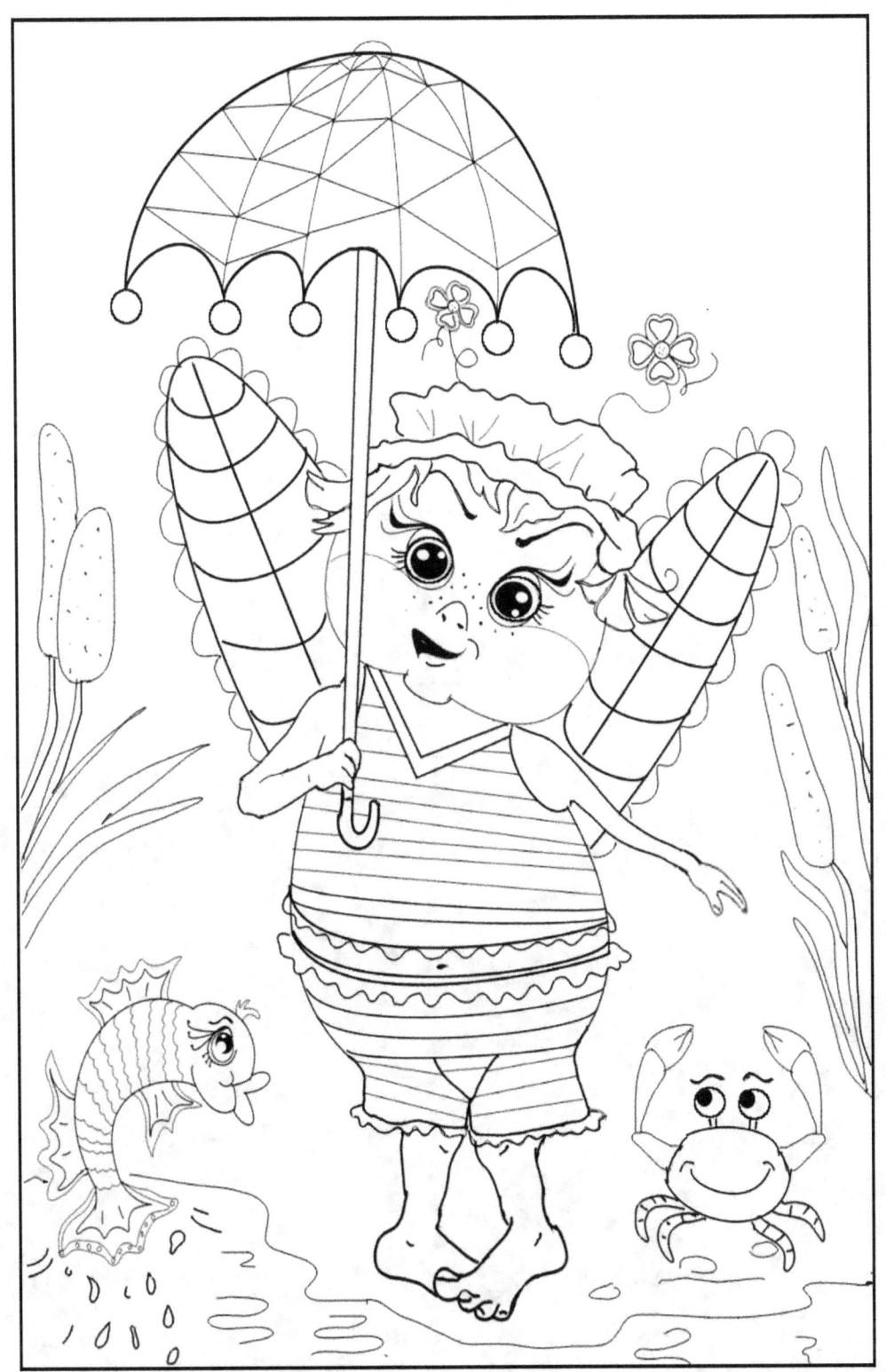

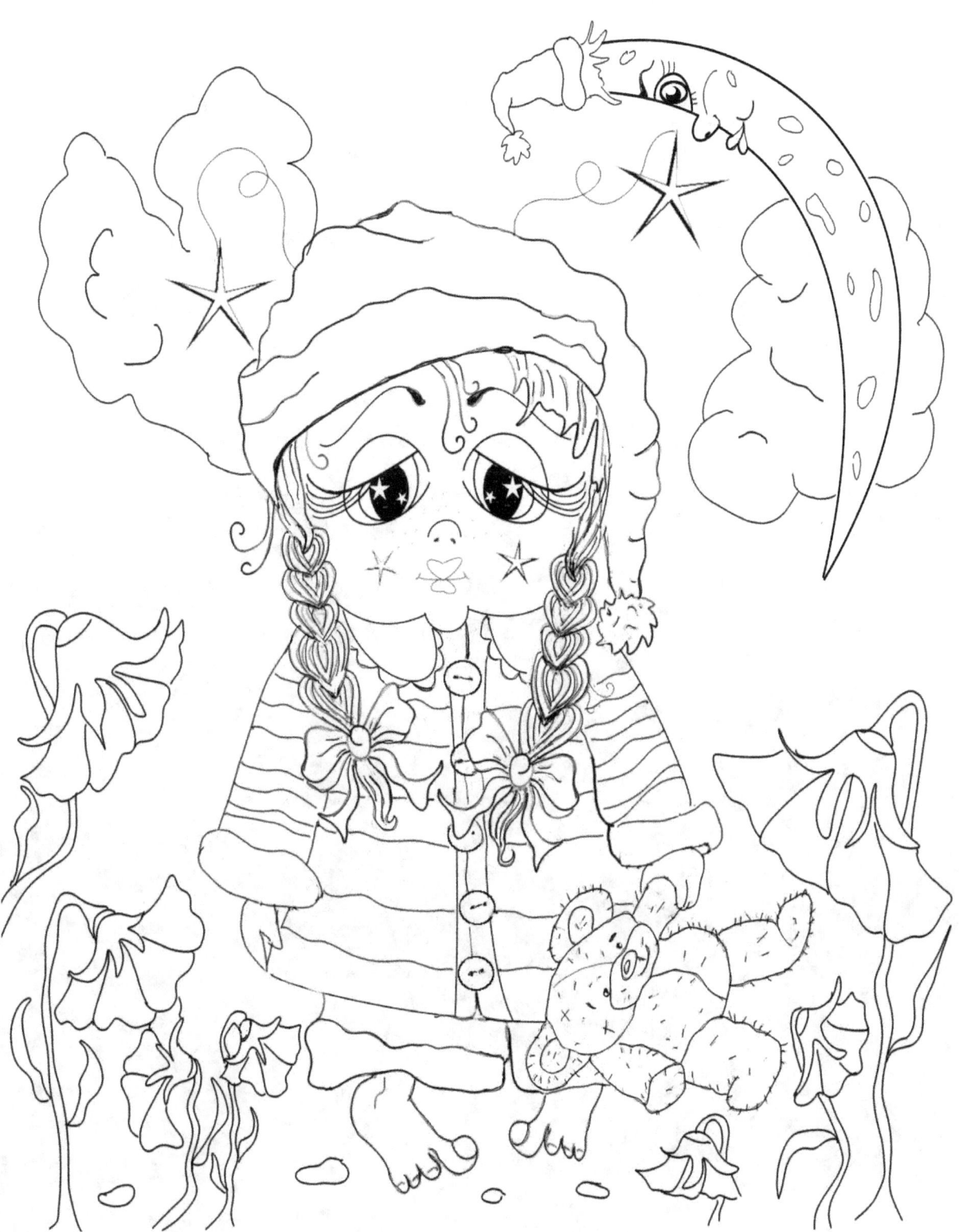

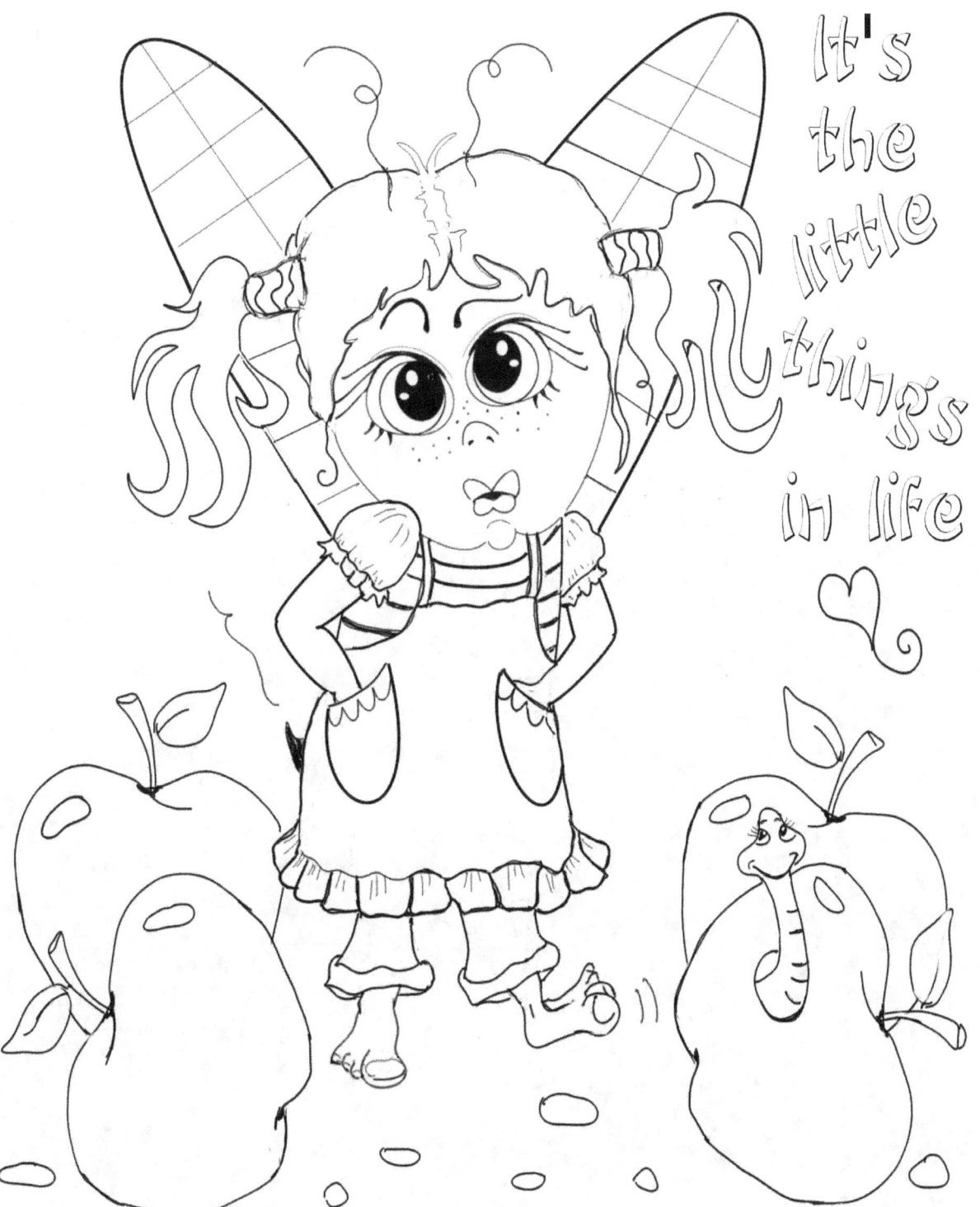

It's
the
little
things
in life

21

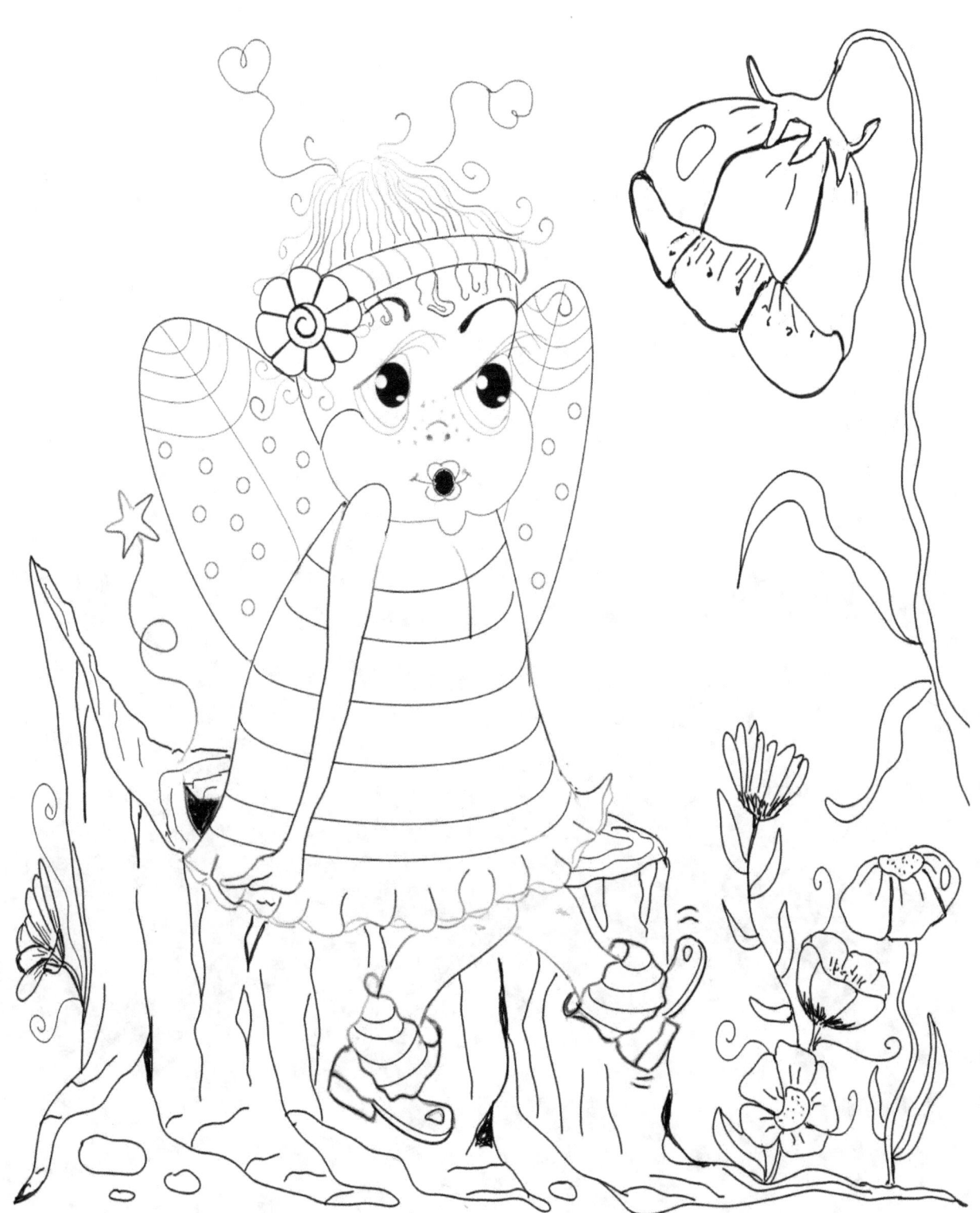

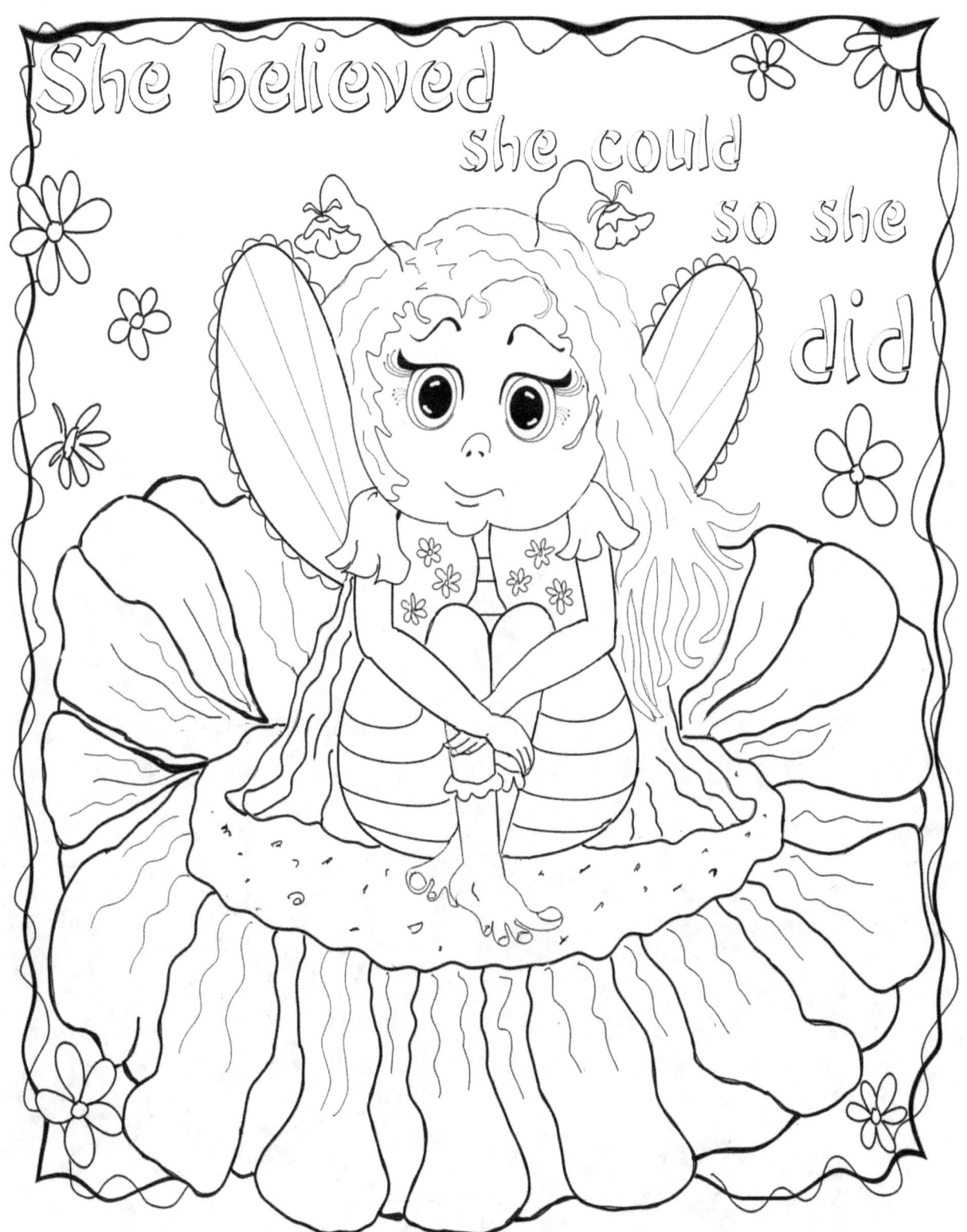

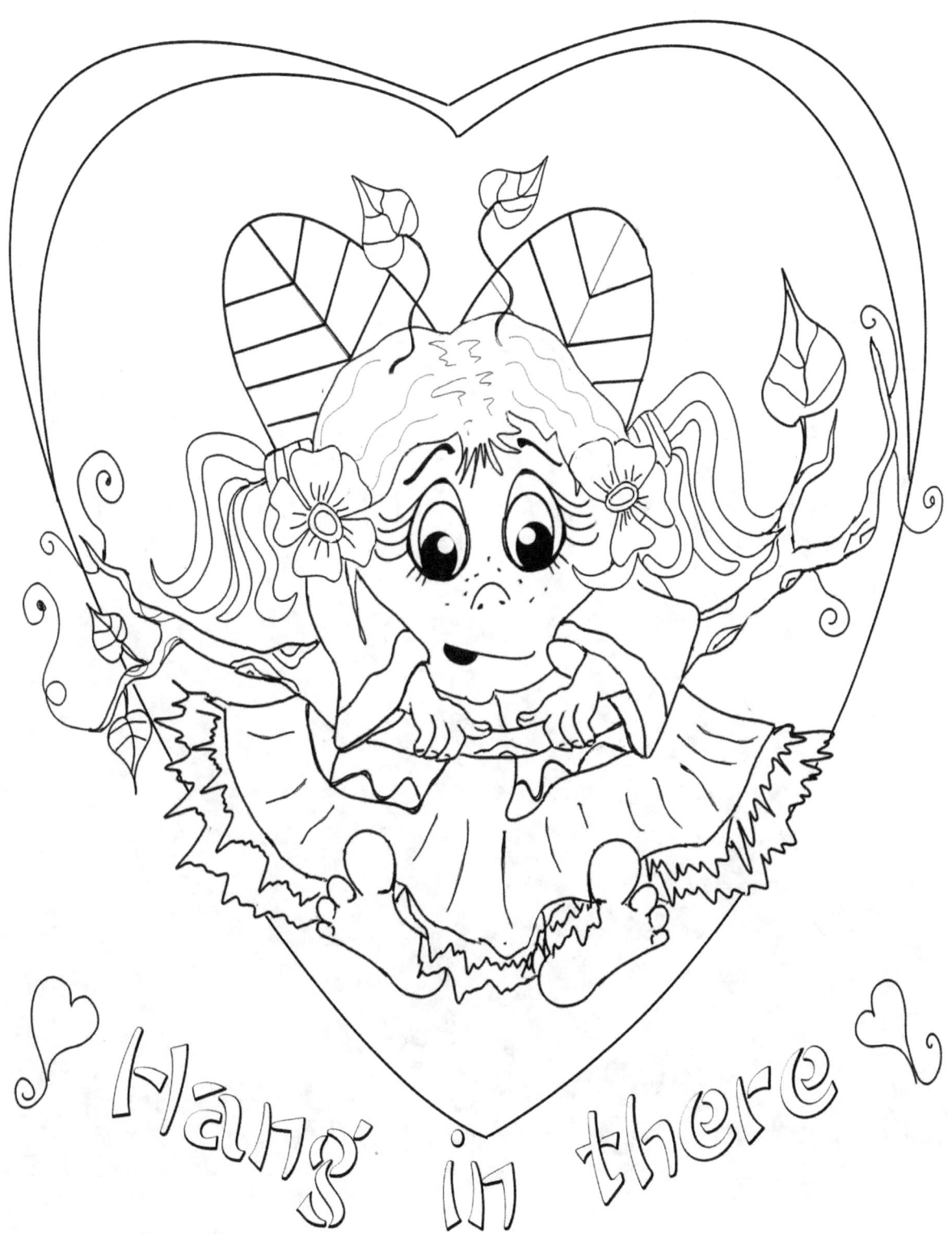

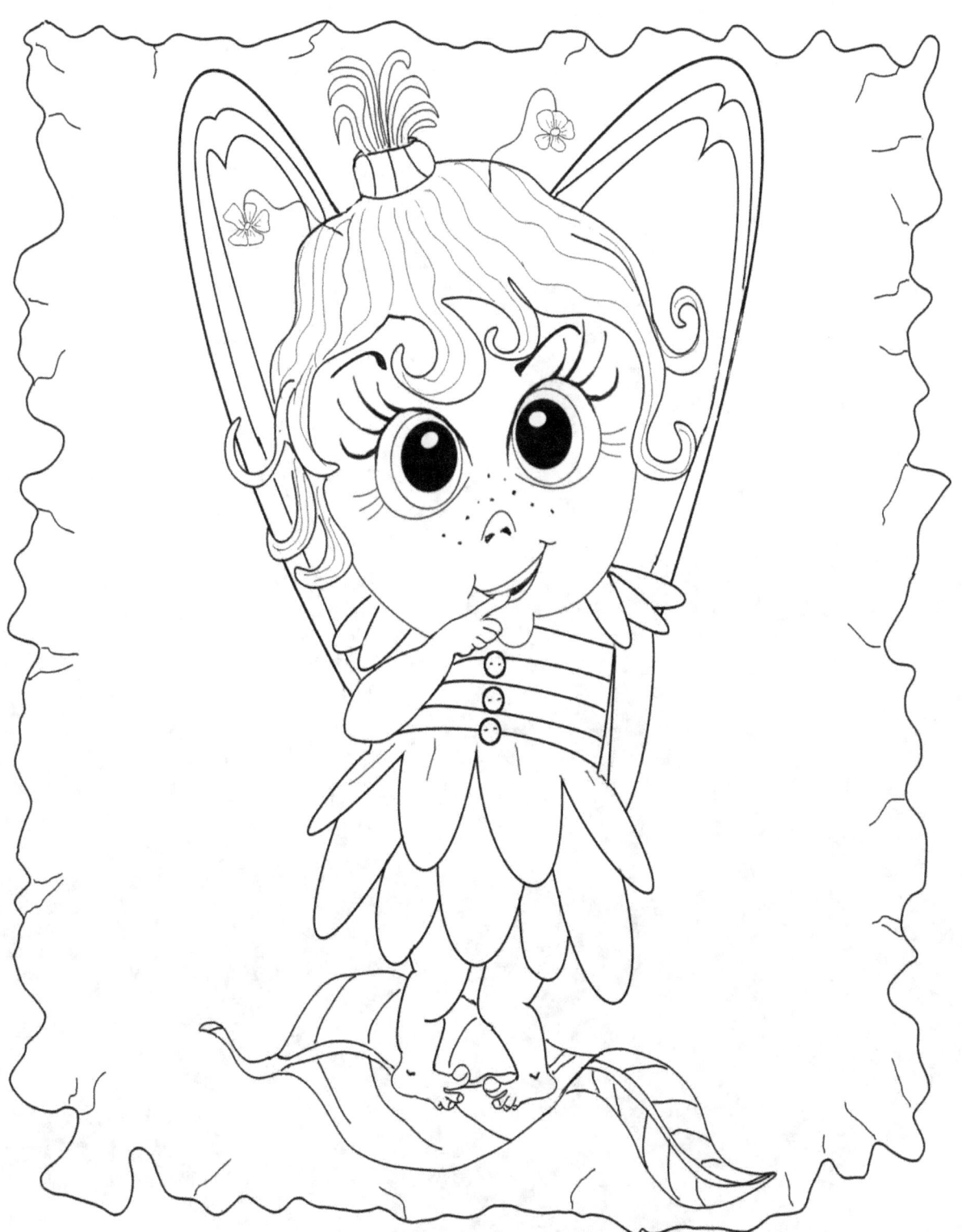

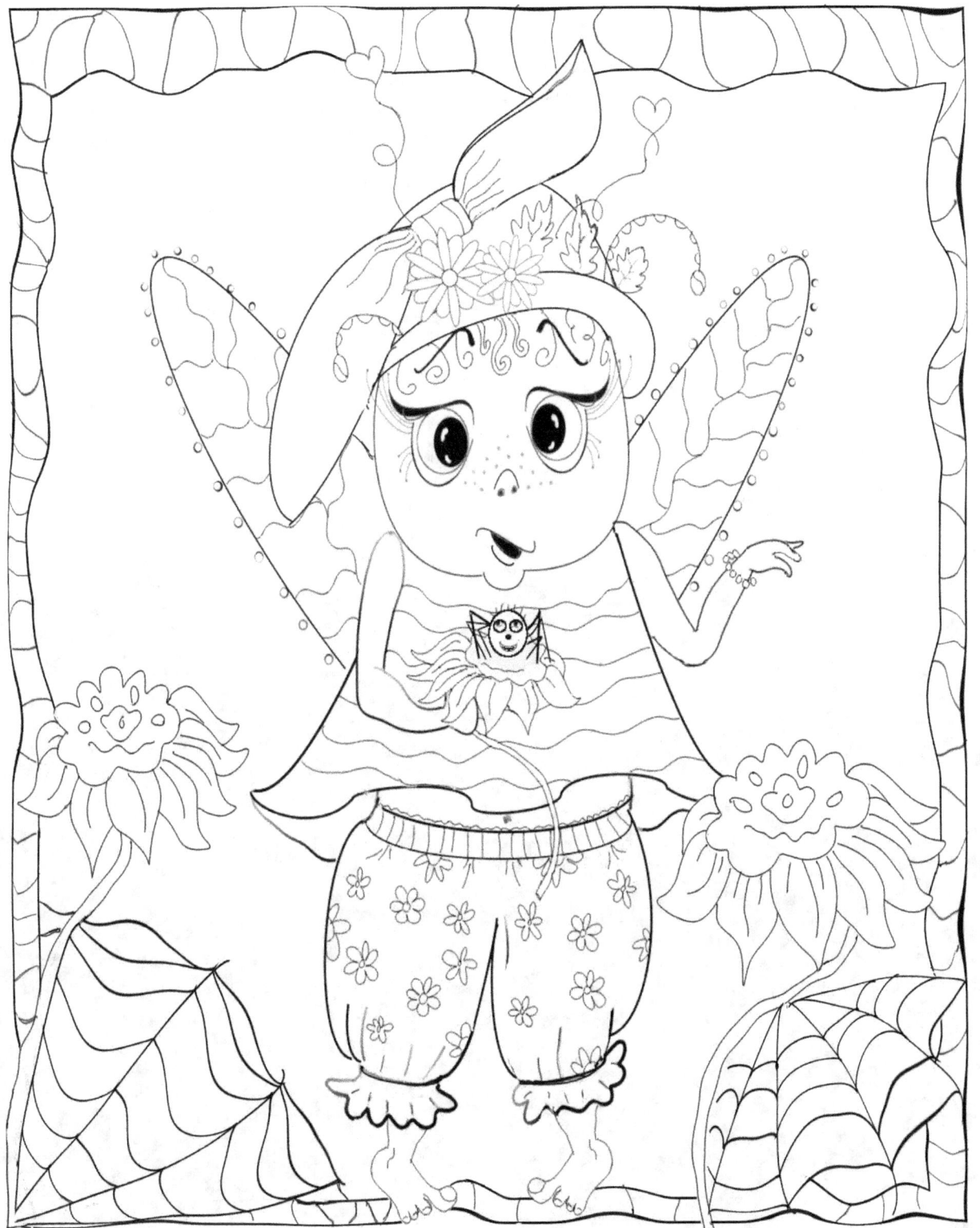

31

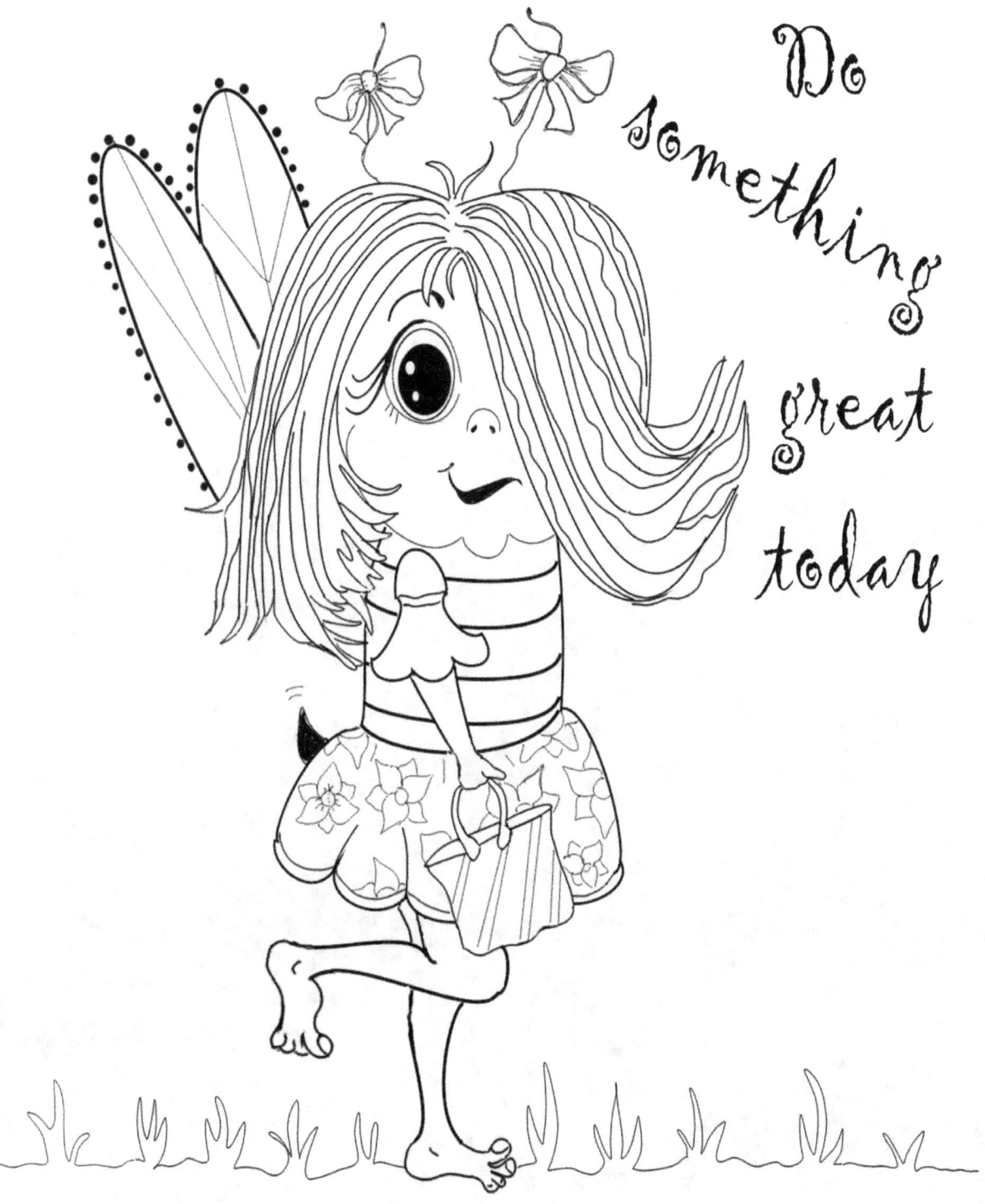

Do
something
great
today

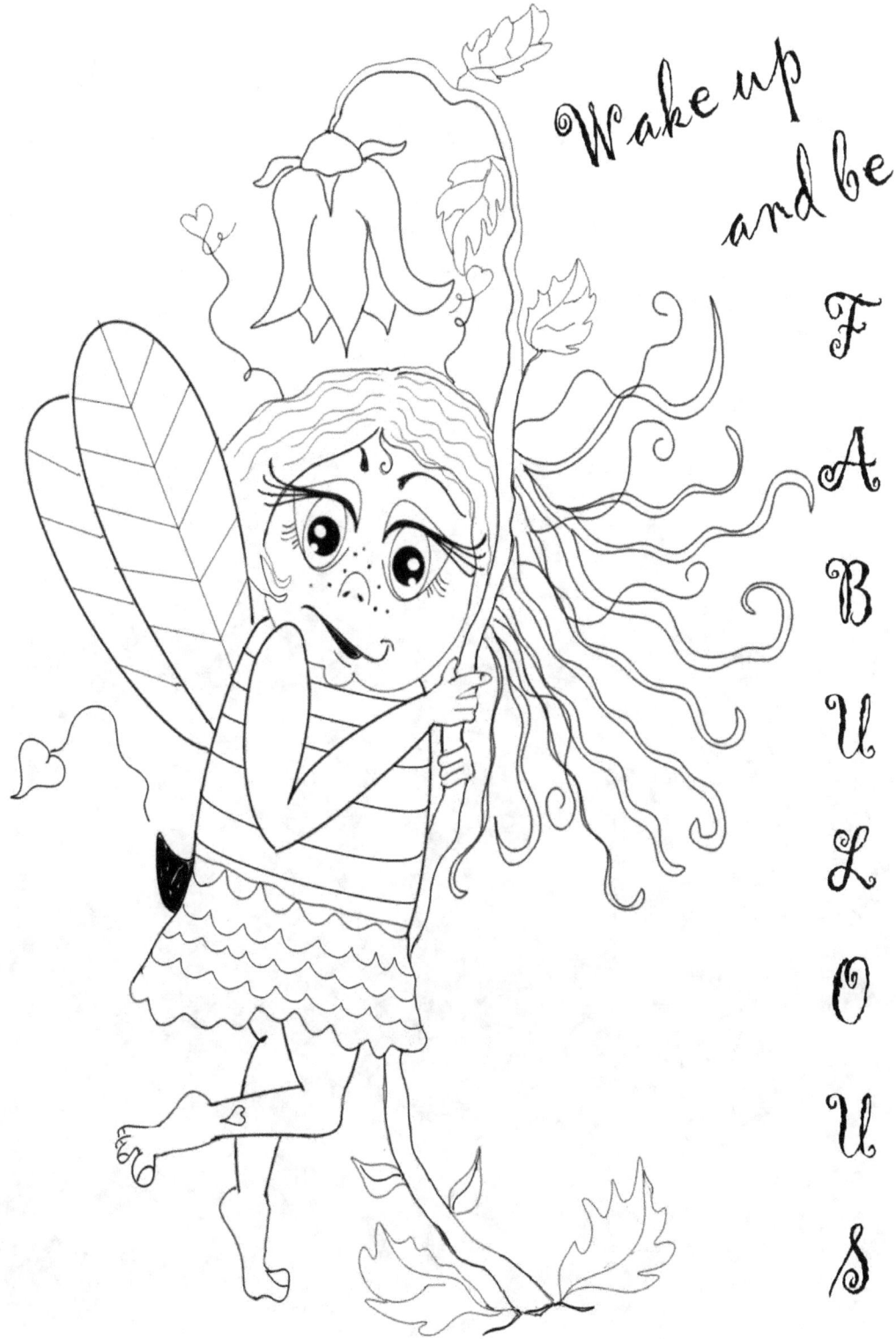

Wake up and be FABULOUS

35

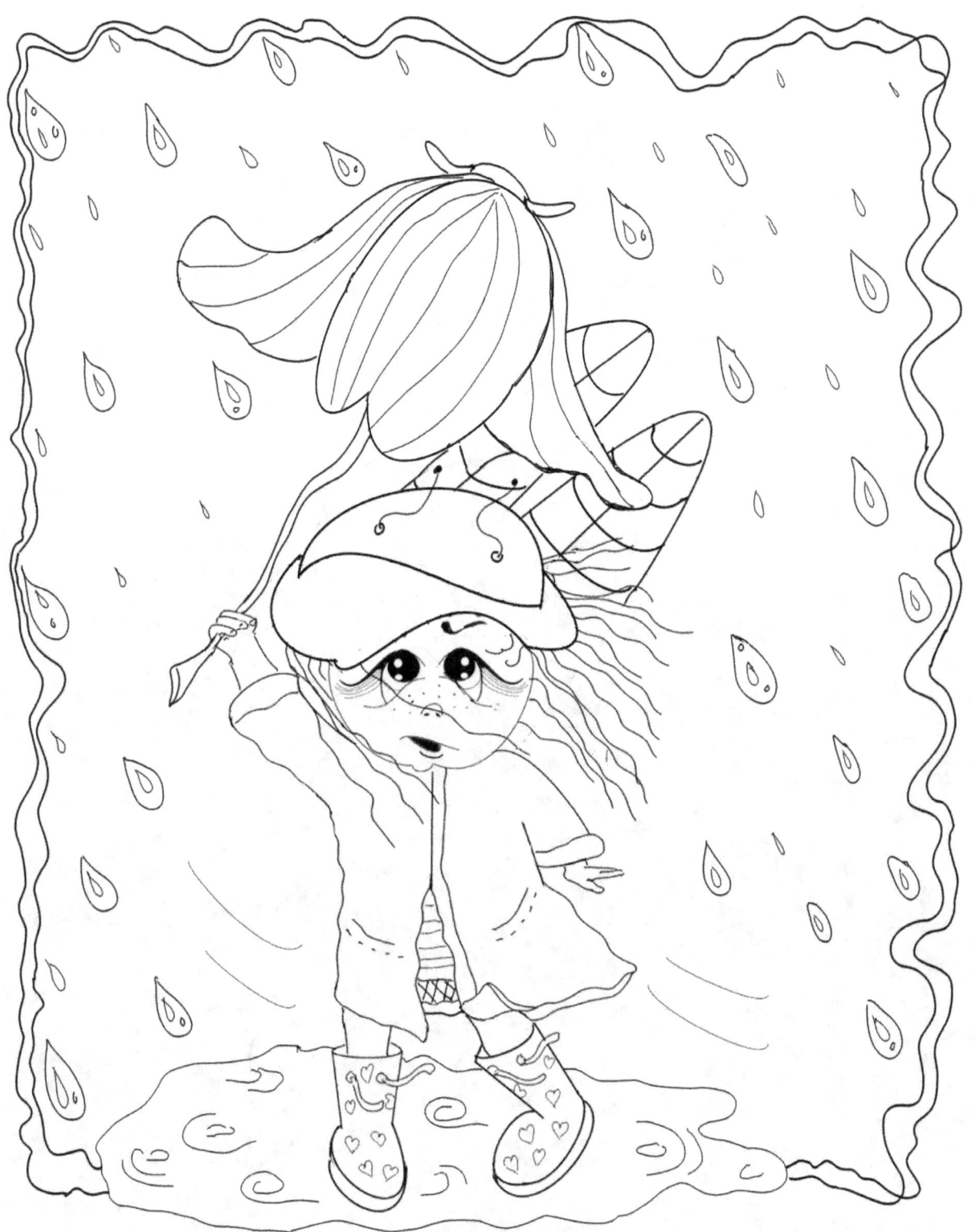

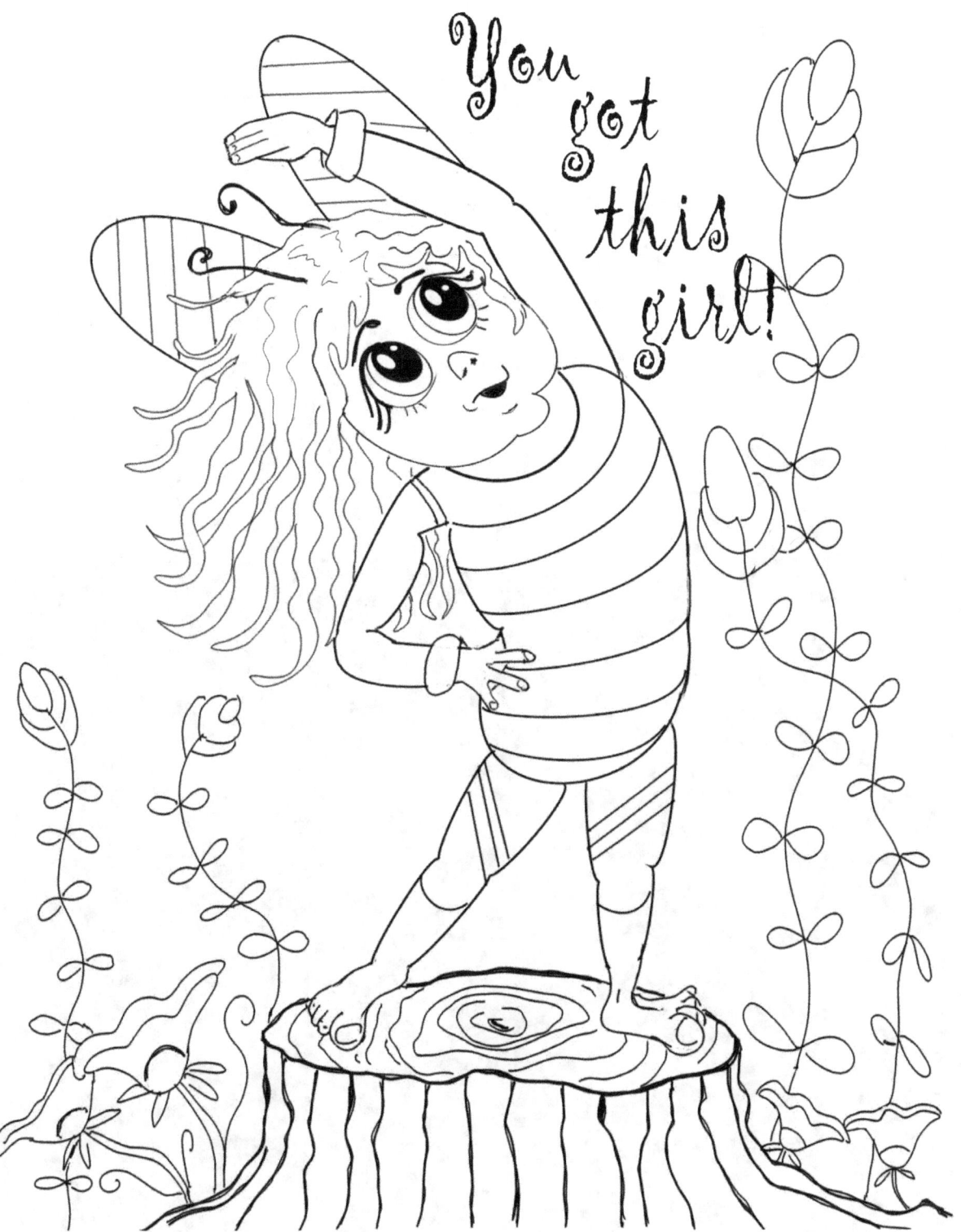

You got this girl!

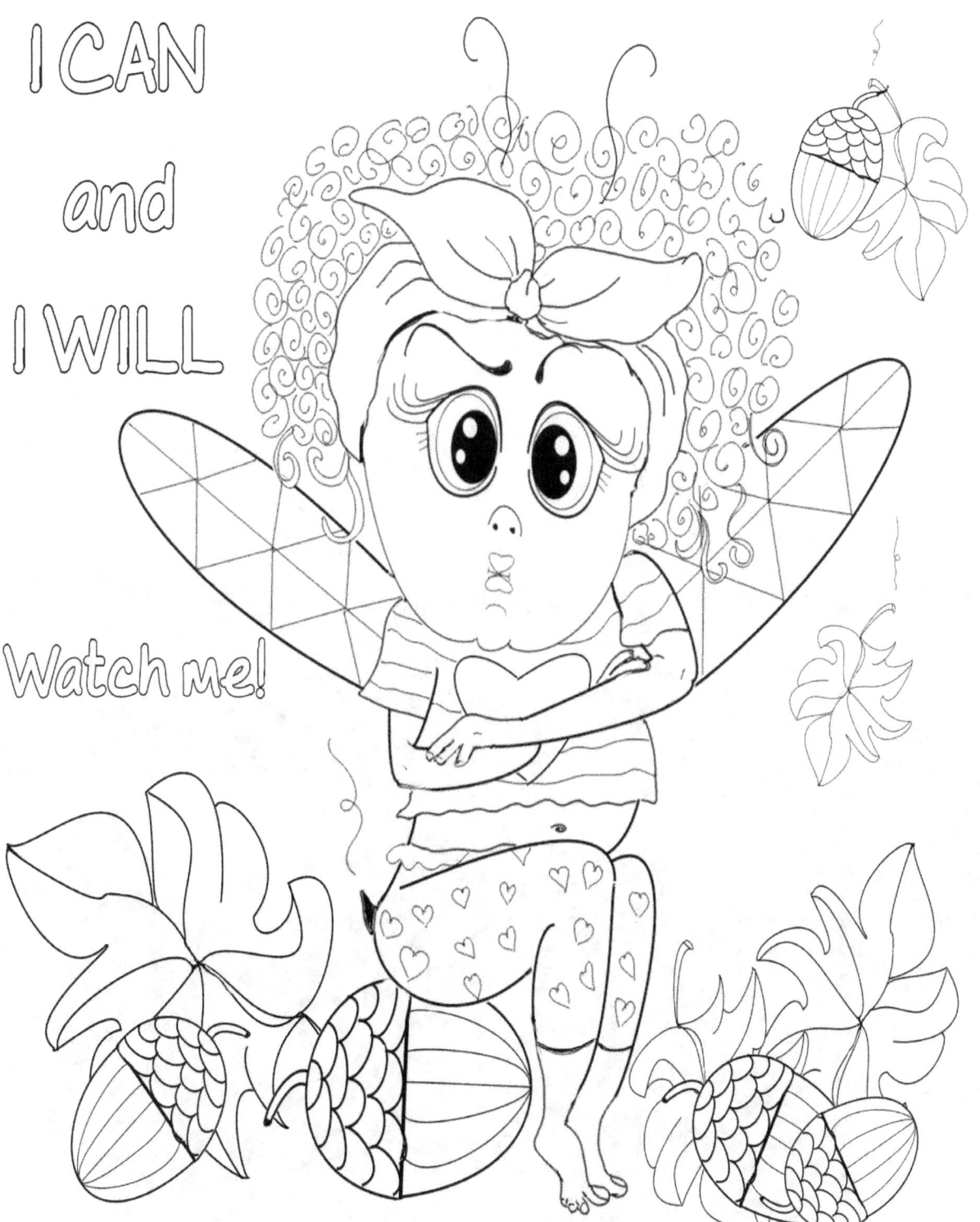

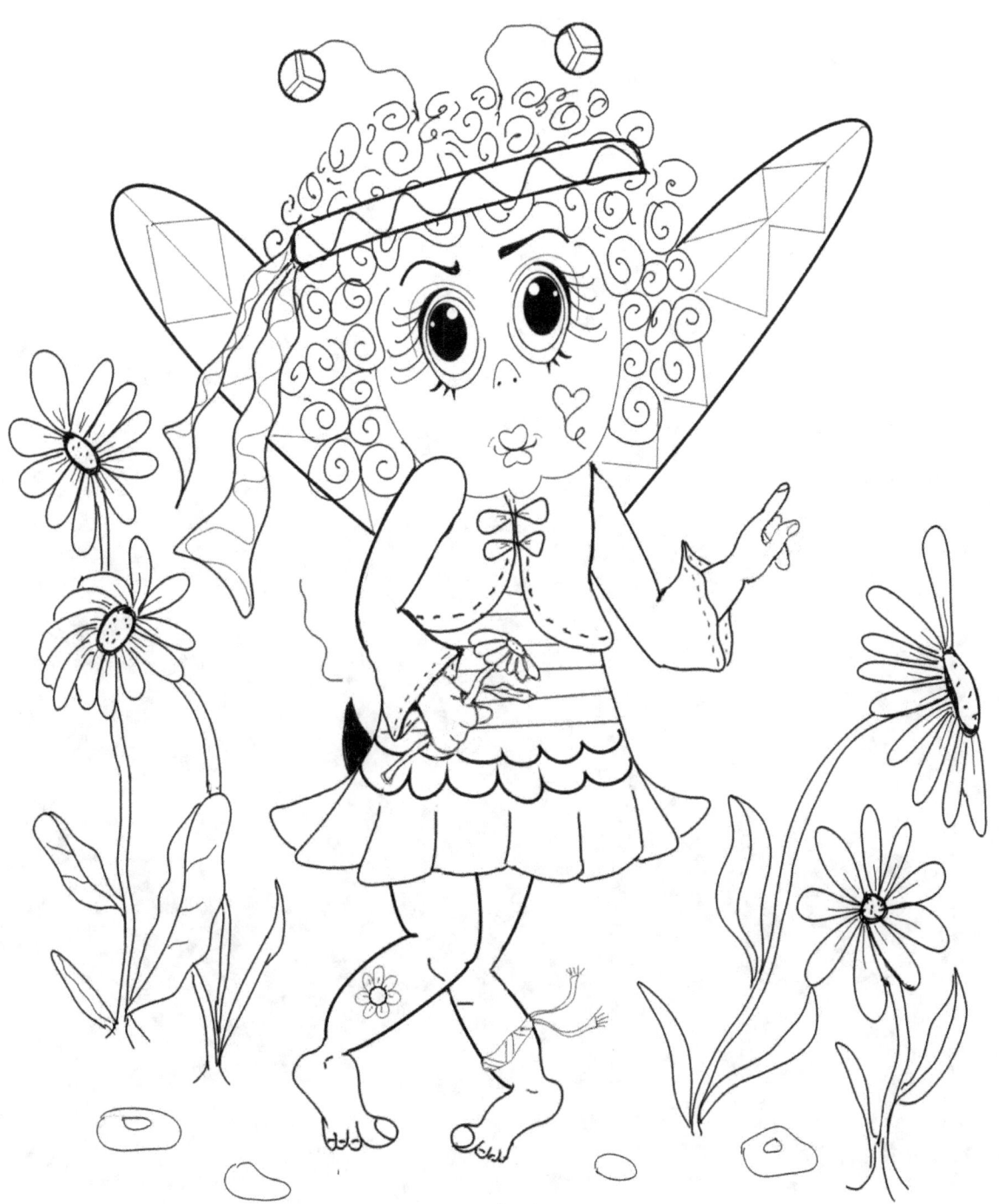

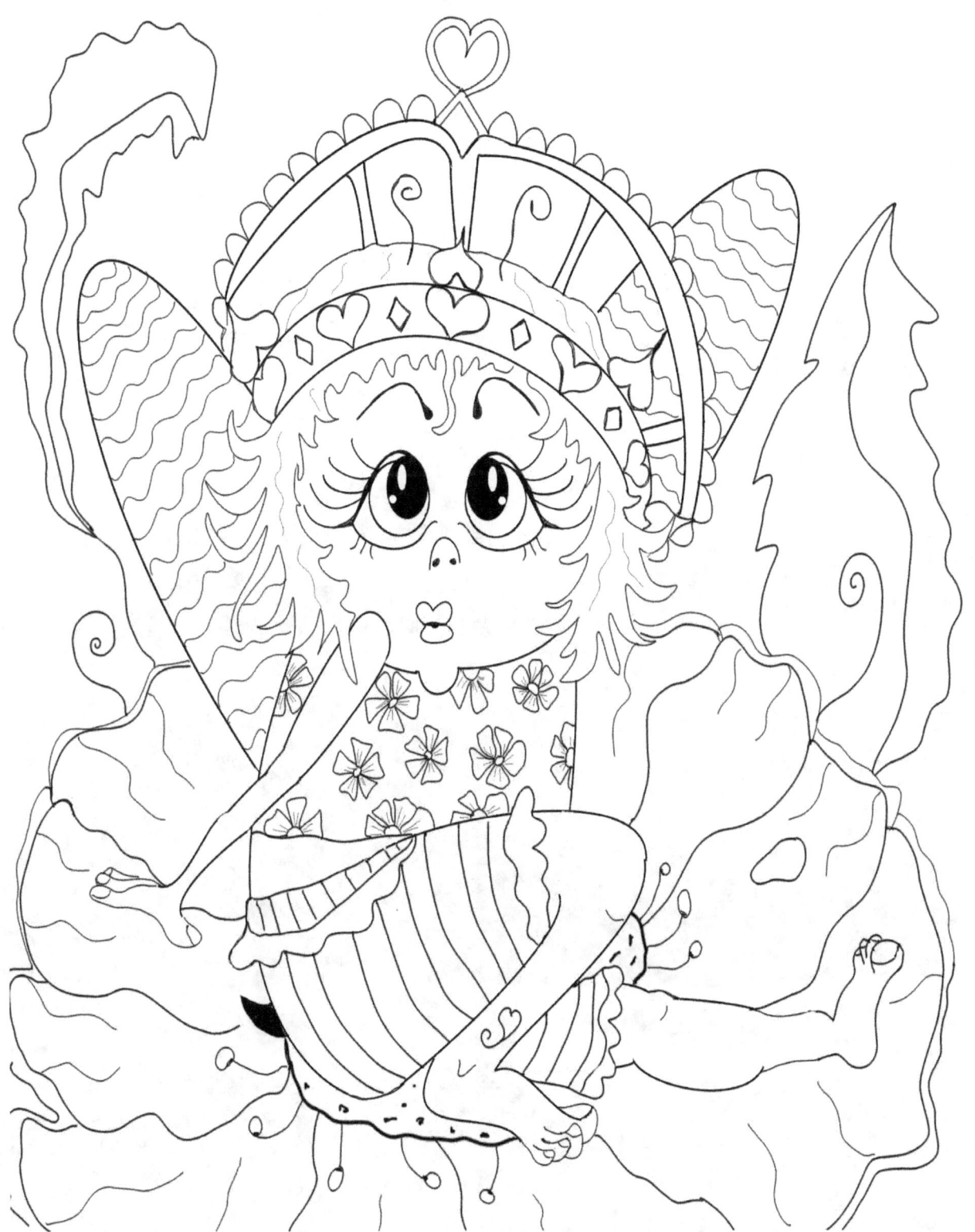

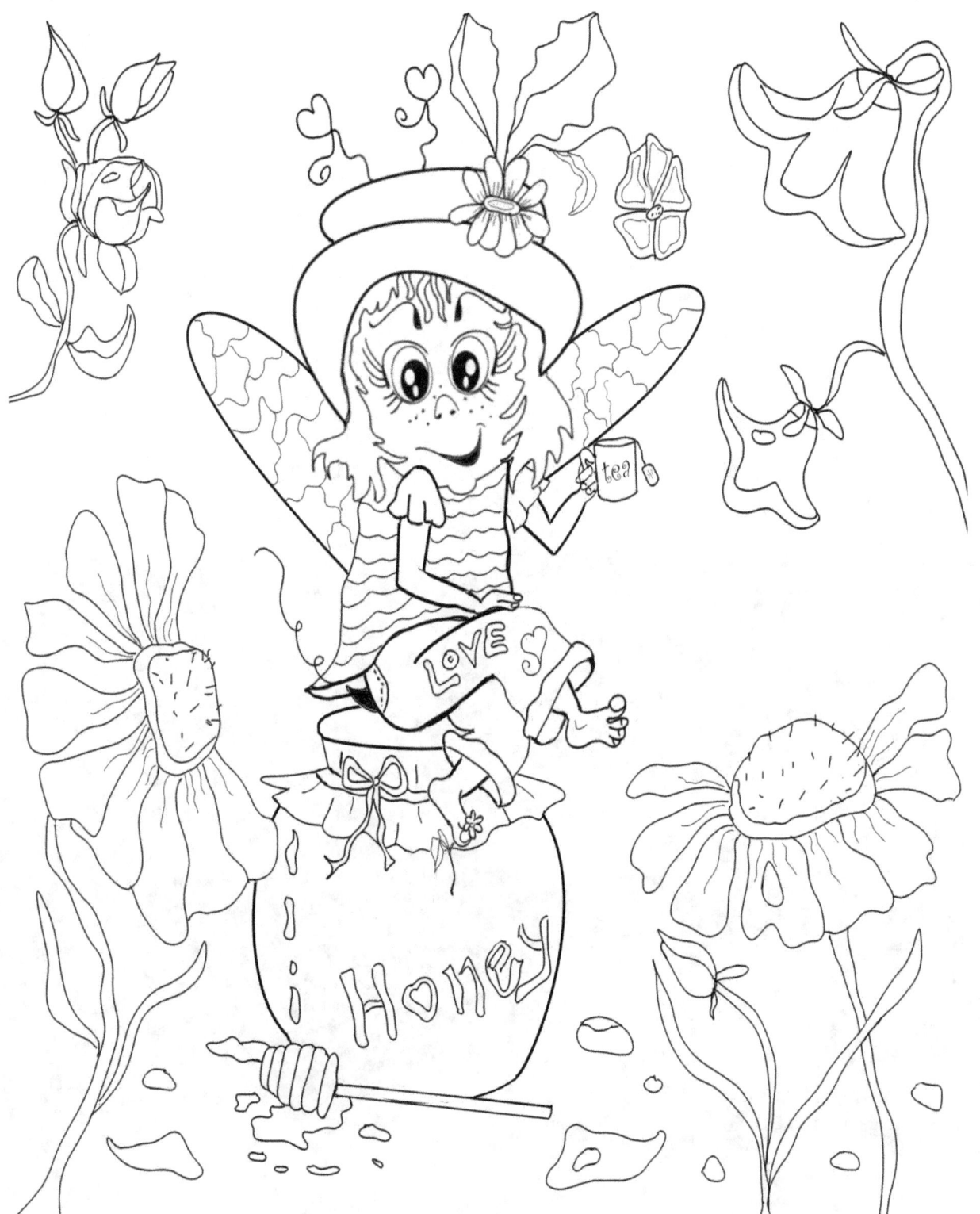

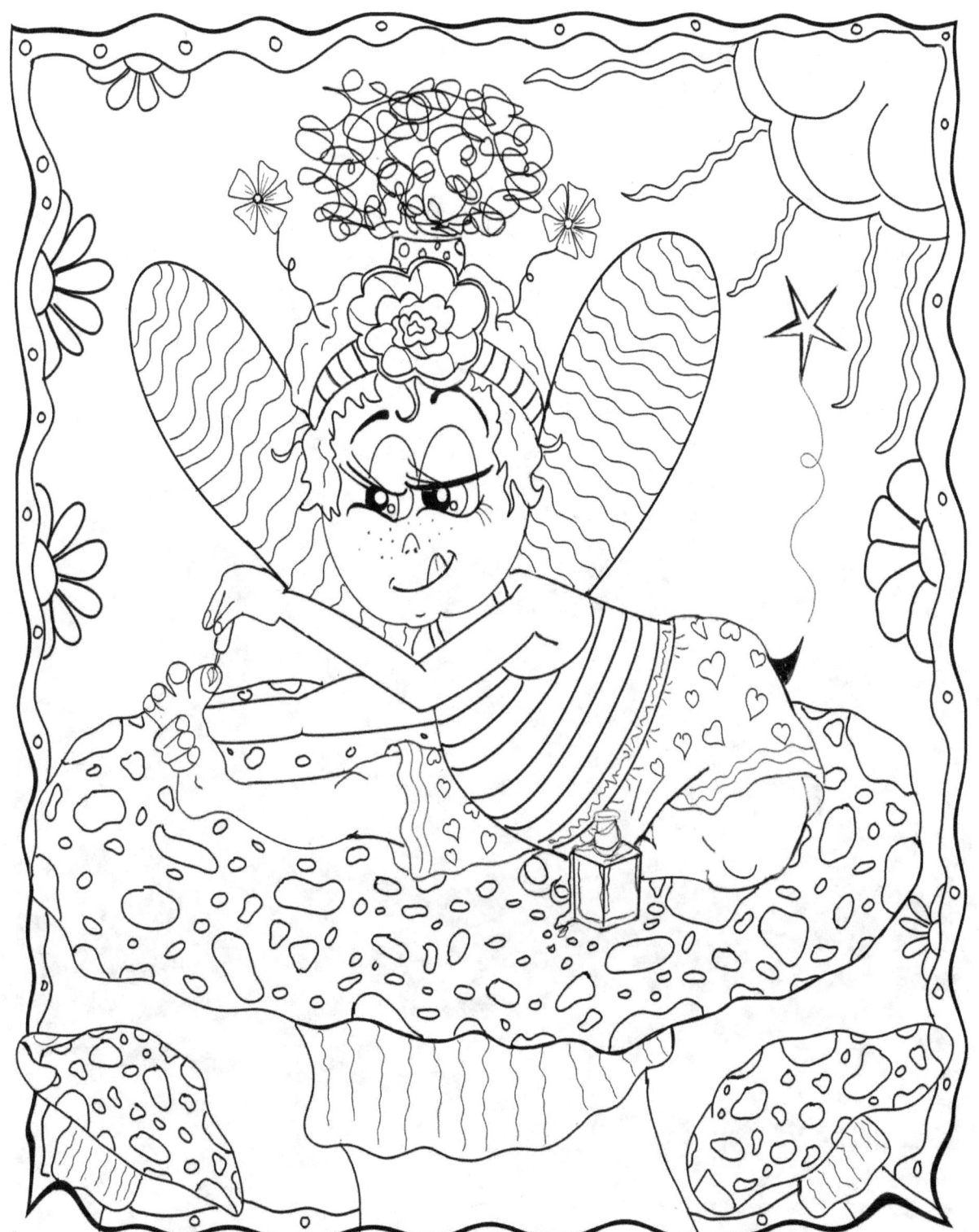

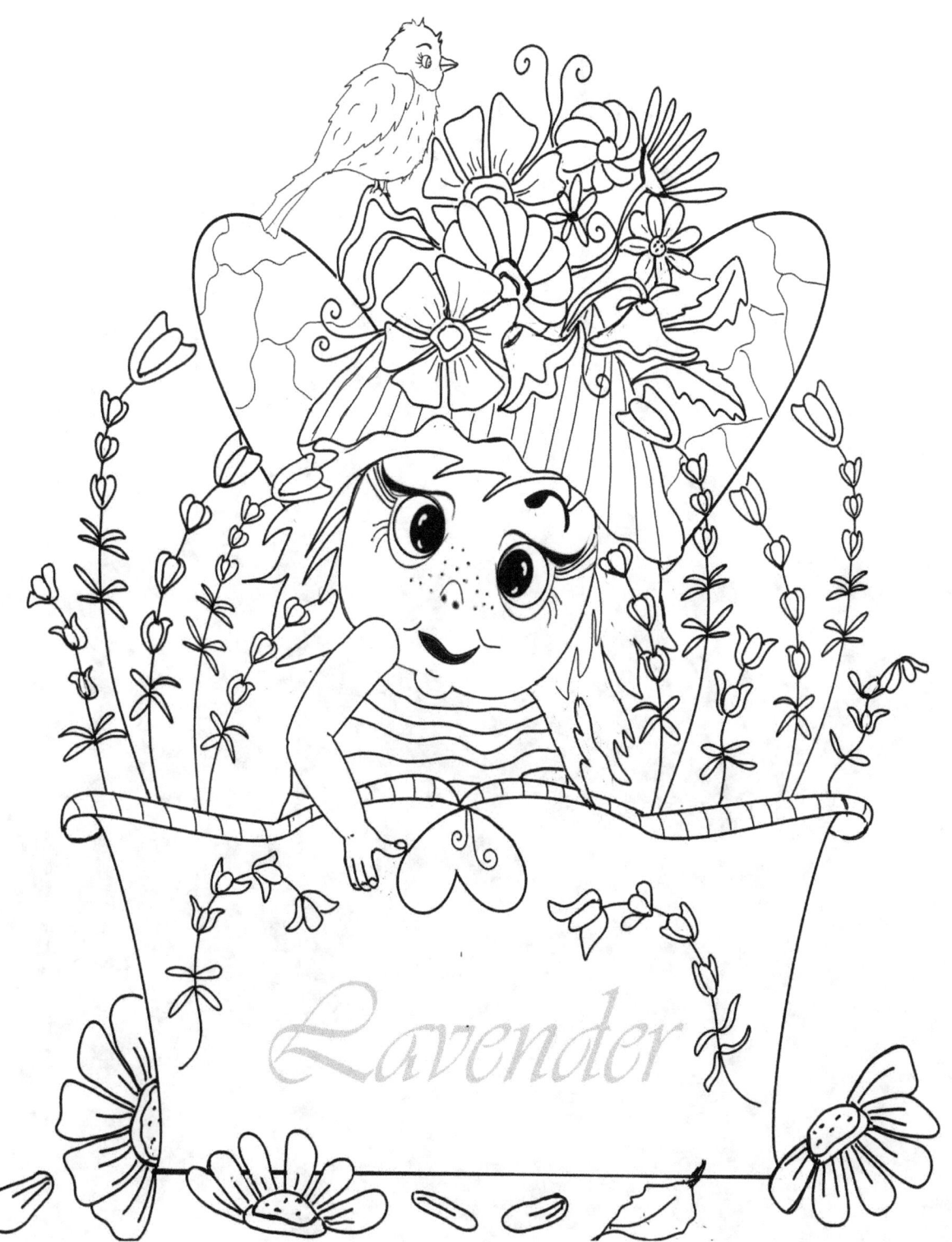

Lavender

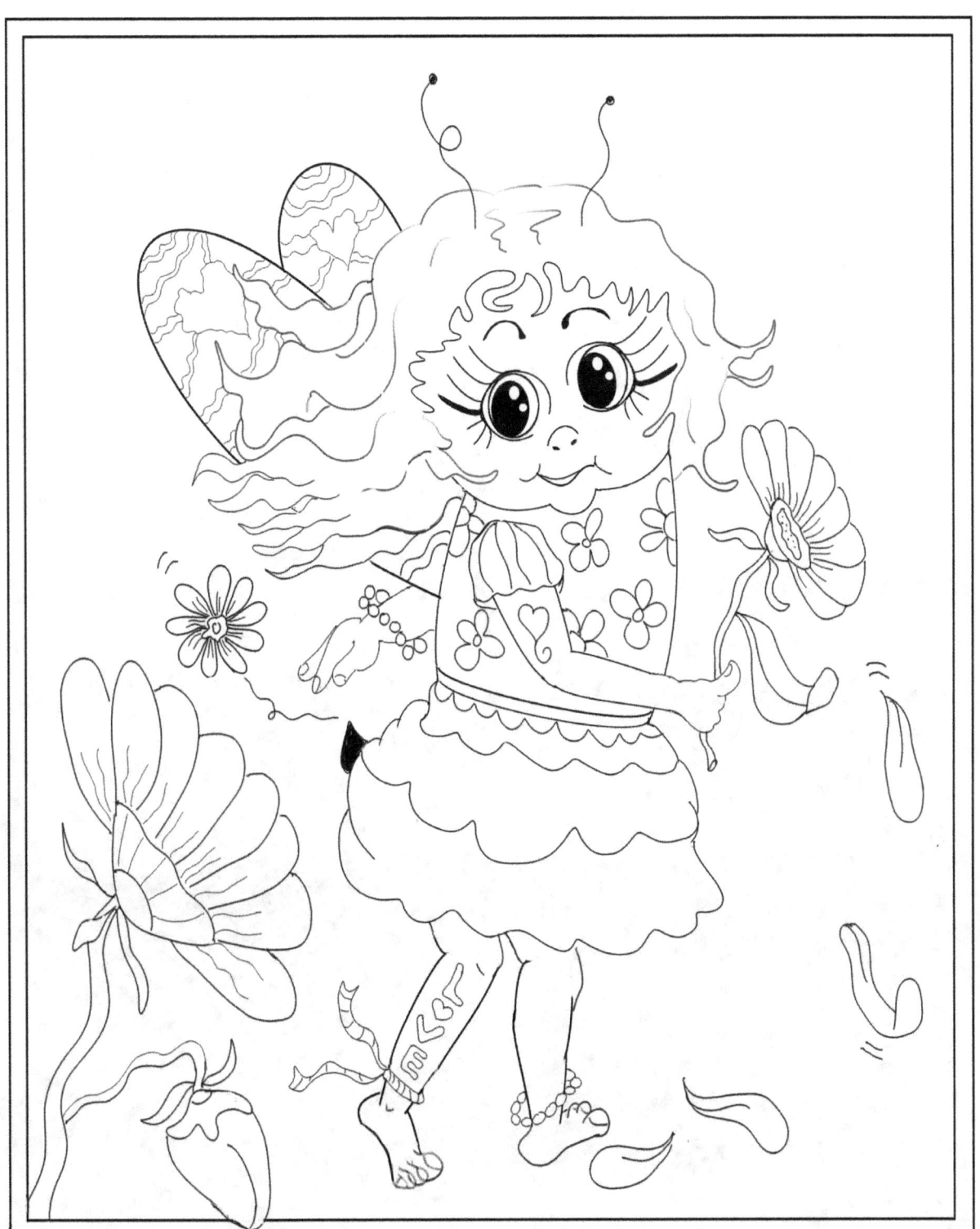

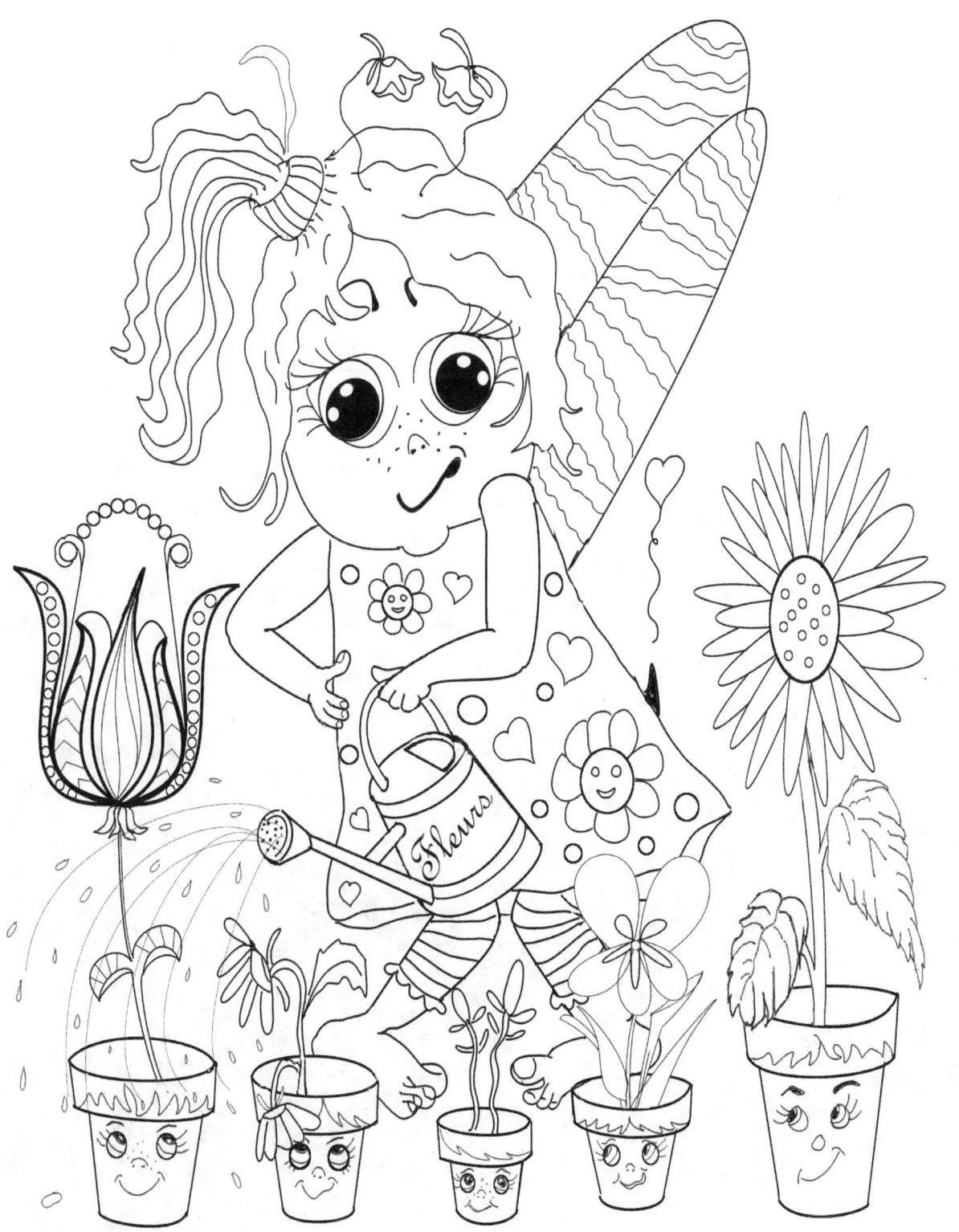

55

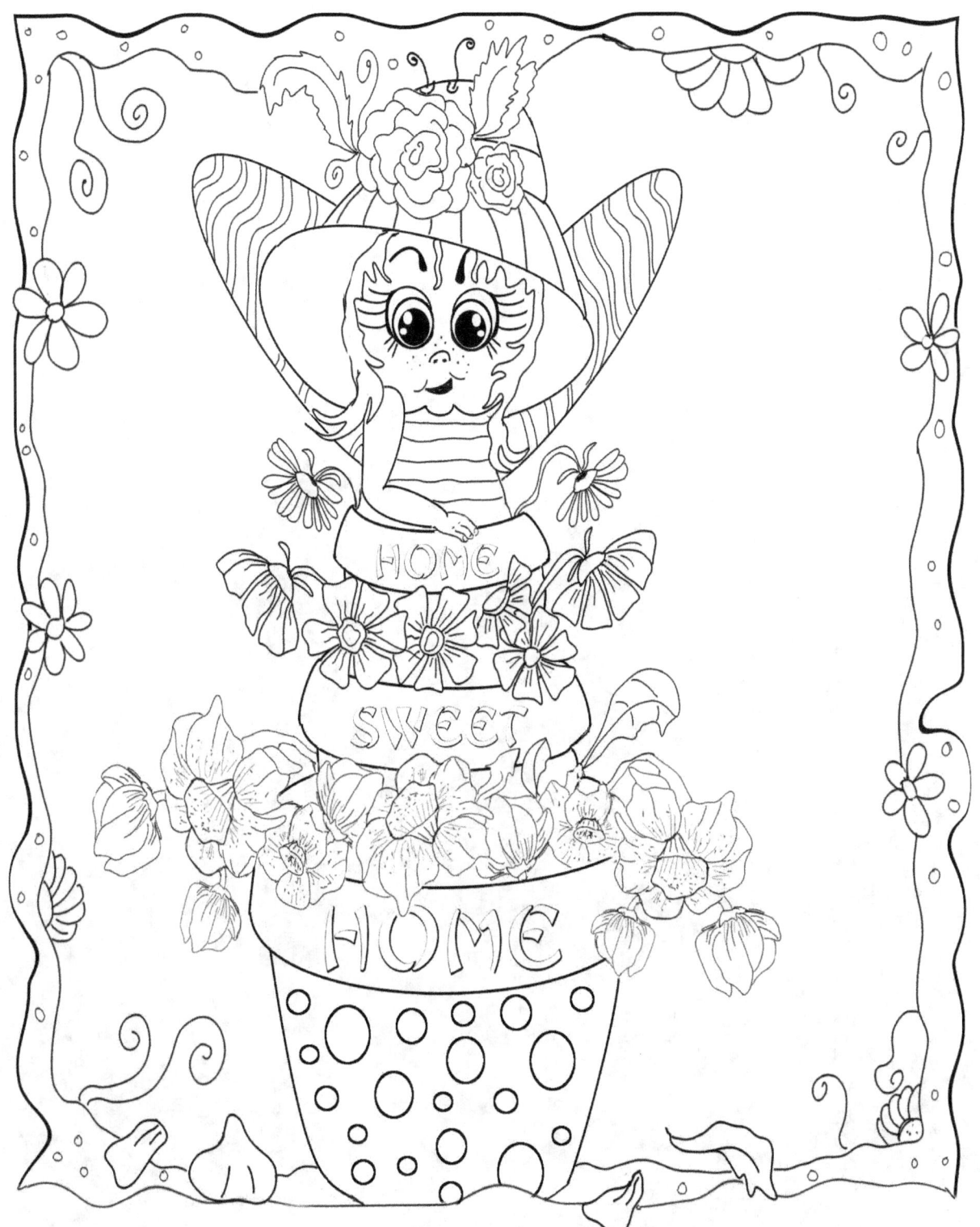

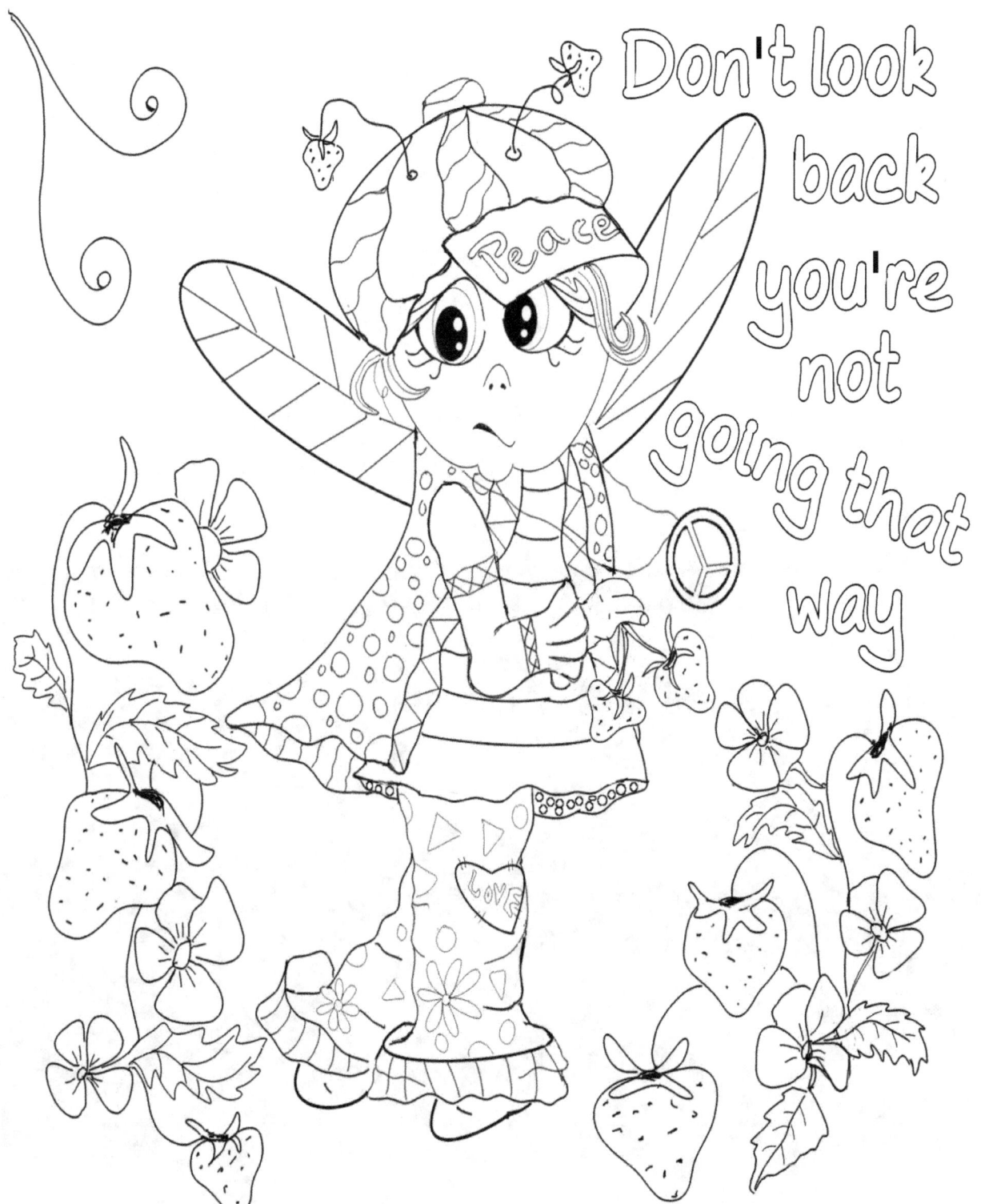

Don't look back you're not going that way